Elements of Dressage

ELEMENTS OF DRESSAGE

A Guide for Training the Young Horse

Kurd Albrecht von Ziegner

CADMOS
EQUESTRIAN

THE AUTHOR

Col. K. A. von Ziegner is known in the equestrian world mainly as a successful trainer. He created both the compelling concept of the "Training Tree" and the Prix St. James, which combines the most important basic dressage requirements with the Prix St. Georges.

The Colonel started his equestrian career as an officer in the German cavalry in 1939. After World War II he became a Licensed Riding Teacher and worked for ten years as Chief Instructor at the University Riding school at Tübingen. During this time, he had many successes in national and international dressage, eventing and jumping competitions at advanced level, eventually being awarded the German Riding Badge in Gold.

In 1956 Col. K. A. von Ziegner was reactivated by the Bundeswehr and became a Commanding Officer of German NATO Forces. Afterwards he was posted for four years to serve as the Chief Instructor at the Turkish Cavalry School in Istanbul, which he reorganized along the lines of the famous German Cavalry School in Hanover.

Since 1971, together with his wife Elisabeth and his son Botho, he has managed a private riding school at Mechtersen near Hamburg. The school also serves as a training centre for the Eventing Division of the German Rider and Driver Association, which he has presided over for more than ten years. Since 1980, Colonel von Ziegner has held dressage clinics and seminars in many countries, mainly in the United States up to Grand Prix.

He has frequently written articles for the German equestrian press, collaborating on the book Deutsche Reitlehre *(Principles of Riding) and became an editor of several editions of Müseler´s* Riding Logic. *In 1995 he published the concept of the "Training Tree" with his first book in the English language,* The Basics.

Copyright of original edition © 2002 by Cadmos Verlag
This edition © 2002 by Cadmos Equestrian
Design by Ravenstein + Partner with a photo of Bruno Baumann
Printed by Westermann Druck Zwickau

ISBN 3-86127-902-9

TABLE OF CONTENTS

To my wife Elisabeth,
who tolerated my absence twice a year.

To my children and grandchildren,
of whom I am proud.

To my horses, who taught me.

FOREWORD

Col. K. Albrecht von Ziegner was not known to me until he attended one of the Training and Teaching Seminars which were held at Tristan Oaks each summer under the auspices of the United States Dressage Federation Welcomed as an observer, he watched a whole day of teaching sessions. During this time a green horse was causing some trouble for his rider. At the end of the day Col. von Ziegner asked permission to ride the horse. Permission was granted, he mounted and walked away on the soft rein. The horse became relaxed and perceptive to the aids. Moving into the trot he presented a very nice movement. As seeing is believing, I wanted the opportunity to learn more about this person. During a lengthy conversation I learned that our ideas about training corresponded closely. I was impressed with his classical methods and his compassion for the horse.

My association with Col. von Ziegner in the years that followed our first meeting has always been in a clinic situation. His approach to rider problems was helpful, and the results proved beneficial for both the rider and the horse. It was enlightening to see the ease with which the corrections were made.

Two helpful ideas were introduced by Col. von Ziegner to our riders. First was the diagram of the Training Tree, which showed schematically the correct steps in the development of the horse, and which also show the time element necessary for the learning process. Col. von Ziegner insists that a correctly trained horse should be able to perform the high-level and the low-level work equally well. The second idea was the Prix St. James test, which he developed to this end, which is now used in competitions in the areas where he has done a good deal of work with both riders and horses.

During the years I have observed Col. von Ziegner´s work in the United States and learned more about his equestrian philosophy, I have gained respect for his ability to direct his students towards the correct understanding of what dressage training should mean to them. This book will spread his teachings throughout the country and will, I believe, contribute greatly to the education of our dressage riders.

Violet Hopkins
Tristan Oaks
White Lake, Michigan, † 2002

INTRODUCTION

Everyone knows that dressage is not teaching tricks to the horse to be shown in the ring. Dressage is the mental and physical training that aims for the full harmony between rider and horse. Though it is fascinating, dressage is primarily hard work, demanding self-discipline and fairness towards the horse.

The Elements of Dressage and the Training Tree are not a "new school". What I have in mind is to help trainers and riders better to comprehend the German way of training a horse, which emphasizes the importance of a solid foundation. It is the systematic elements of basic training that enable the horse later to be successful in international competitions.

The German approach, which is practised in most countries, is not a new school either, as it is an outgrowth of the Classical School developed by the old masters. It has been published in *Deutsche Reitlehre*, the official handbook for German instructors, and it has been translated into English as *The Principles of Riding and Advanced Techniques of Riding*.

The Elements of Dressage is meant to be a complement to these standard German manuals. However, there are some important distinctions. The concept of the Training Tree was developed out of over 50 years of my experience training horses and riders. In that time I became convinced that certain aspects of the German Training Scale need to be thought about in a different way and revised in some aspects. When the German Training Scale was conceived I both contributed to and endorsed it. A lifetime of work and reflection resulted in the Training Tree, first published in „The Basics" in the United States.

The Training Tree is meant to simplify and clarify the complex issue of training. It should give the reader the right perspective on training as well as answer the following questions:
• What are the essential elements of dressage?
• How do we achieve these elements?
• In what order do we develop these elements in training?
• What is the purpose of the movements and school figures?
• When are these movements useful? When are they harmful or even damaging?
• How do we introduce these movements to the horse?

The Elements of Dressage will help clarify misconceptions in training a horse. In addition to the above-mentioned standard manuals, it is a guide for everyone who wants to train a young horse up to the higher levels in dressage as well as jumping or eventing.

The procedure may take time, but in basic training, the longer way is actually the shorter one, as the horse's well-being is prerequisite and the key to success.

THE UNALTERABLE PRINCIPLES

"The horse is God's gift to mankind."
(Arabian Proverb)

When you set out to build a house, you certainly would start with a solid foundation. The importance of such a solid base for your structure will increase with each storey you add.

When planting a tree from which you expect to harvest tasty and healthy fruits, you prune it down in its early years to make the trunk strong, stable and long-lived.

These are the images you should have in mind when training a young horse. Since you want your horse to stay in lasting good health, you need a solid foundation that enables your horse to perform successfully when matured. You must proceed with care, developing the mental and physical abilities of your horse systematically in a natural way.

Sounds logical? After all, there is no sense in having a 12-year-old child doing the same things adults are supposed to do. Agreed?

There are several stages a horse has to pass through before it starts with serious training. During the first six months of its life, the foal is well cared for by its mare. In addition, the breeder does his or her best to accustom the foal to humans. The next stage is kindergarten, where the yearling receives special care since there are new experiences and challenges, many of them potentially harmful.

A young horse spends the first three and a half years of its life among its comrades. The breeder has worked hard to produce an animal with excellent physical constitution and by this time, the green horse should be well on its way to domestication. It should be familiar with a lead rope, being tied, a bridle, a saddle, a lunge line, a trailer, and, of course, the farrier. A young horse that is sound and self-confident is ready for the next step – its training.

Fig. 1

Now it is up to you, the trainer to take on this job. What a great feeling and challenge! But are you sure you know how to go about it? Let us talk about it first.

You are a knowledgeable horseperson and you have seen a lot of horses trained by good, not so good, and sometimes even bad trainers. You want to be a good trainer.

Let's assume your horse is a three-and-a-half-year old warmblood gelding. At this age the young horse is similar to a ten-year-old child and is expected to grow up to one more hand in height. Your horse might look big, strong and ready to go, but his bones, joints and ligaments are not yet fully developed. Improper handling (the first danger being the lunge line) can result in serious damage.

With constant care, you start establishing a close relationship with your young horse. He will learn how to behave and how to deal with the new environment you have brought him into. He will learn to understand you just by the sound of your voice and your hand movements. He will also become well aware of the carrot in your pocket. He will learn to distinguish when your voice indicates that you want him to come (your offering hand, Fig. 1), from when your voice indicates that you want him to go (your hand raising the stick).

Before long, your horse will learn to accept your authority just has he respects the leader of the herd. Some people do not understand this and confuse the horse rather than gain his confidence. Once the horse has found out that he is superior in strength (or intelligence), he may cause problems whenever he feels like

it – a serious setback in training. Do not handle your horse like a pet dog or a person. Handle him like a horse. Study his character and mind. Horses are always horses. They think like horses and they act like horses.

Their original community is the herd. Their defence is flight. If they are afraid or spooky, it is because they are horses! Forgive them as they will forgive you.

Horses do not have a lot of brains, but they are not stupid. They just do not think the way humans think. Their actions are instant and spontaneous, not a result of various logical considerations.

Horses have amazing instincts and are capable of great sensitivity, beyond the human imagination. They can feel an earthquake hours in advance. They also have excellent memory. They do not forget frightening experiences. Instincts coupled with memory may explain why a frightened, nervous horse cannot be calmed down as quickly as one would wish. This aspect of a horse´s nature must always be of primary consideration, and must always be handled with a great deal of patience.

But it is not only the bad experiences they remember. Horses don't forget good experiences, either. For example, horses can always find their way back to the stable.

Horses are born good-natured. Bad characters are developed through human failures in training. A horse easily adopts bad manners if the human responsible for him is not consistent with the following of rules for handling horses.

The horse must trust you. Do not expect love. The more you understand your horse – his personality as well as his problems – the easier it will be to achieve friendship and collaboration.

Always aim for a partnership with your horse by creating harmony, confidence, and willingness. Always be honest and fair towards your horse. Never overreact! Discipline yourself before you discipline your horse.

When you ask your horse for a response, always use proper execution of the request. When the horse responds as expected, tell him he is a good boy. Never ask for more than the horse is able to give, for this may damage his confidence. Remember, we don't ask for perfection, we strive to it.

Sometimes it is wiser to give in a little in order to gain a lot. But if there is no other choice than breaking serious resistance by force in order to avoid disaster, you must be sure to master the situation. Otherwise, you´d better leave it up to a more effective and courageous rider.

Remember, the horse is stronger than you. Once he finds out that resistance may be a way to evade your control or even frighten you, you have lost a good part of your authority. You must convince the horse to co-operate. The horse must understand what you expect him to do. It´s easier to handle one pound of brain than a thousand pounds of horsepower.

Before starting serious training, take time to reflect on your goal and the way to achieve it. The goal has not changed since the days of the French master François Robichon de la Guérinière (1688–1751), who wrote:

The aim of this noble and useful art is solely to make the horse supple, relaxed, flexible, compliant, and obedient – and to lower the quarters, without all of which a horse whether he be meant for military service [eventing], hunting [jumping], or dressage will neither be comfortable in his movements nor pleasurable to ride.

The *method* has not changed either. It is the procedure of training that follows the principles of classical dressage, which according to the FEI, is:

the harmonious development of the physique and ability of the horse . . . which makes the horse calm . . . supple . . . confident, attentive, and keen, thus achieving perfect understanding with his rider . . . The horse thus gives the impression of doing of his own accord what is required of him. Confident and attentive he submits generously to the control of his rider.

Both definitions mention the essentials of classical dressage that one must deal with not only in the upper levels, but especially in basic training. There is no other way but honest work – no alternative, no modern or old- fashioned way, there is only the right way or the wrong way. The principles of classical dressage are unalterable. It is impossible to change these principles, for they are the foundation of equestrian sport. We must strive to understand and practise these principles correctly at all times.

Fig. 2

Fig. 3

Fig. 4

Fig. 5

The basic training, which is an all-around and comprehensive training, takes about two years. In the first year the horse learns to handle the rider's weight. He learns to move in a relaxed and rhythmic way, maintaining a steady contact with the rider´s hands. He learns to respond to the aids from the seat, legs and hands. Once the horse is on the aids, he can be worked towards First Level. Besides the flatwork, the horse should also be introduced to cross-country work, with small fences, ditches and water.

At the end of the first year, the horse should be confident with his rider. He should be familiar with hacking cross-country as well as in traffic. He should also be able to perform a First Level test as well as a clear round over small stadium fences in an adequate style.

Dressage prospects need only enough jumping to provide variation of the routine (Figs. 2–5).

In the *second* year the horse is on the way to the Second Level. Confirming the First Level movements, the trainer will improve the horse's straightness and start developing the carrying power of the quarters. Without straightness and strength in the hindquarters, Schwung cannot be achieved. At the end of the second year the horse should be ready for

Second Level tests and confident with all kinds of small jumps.

After these two years of *basic training* the horse will be approaching six years of age and will be almost fully grown with his muscles well developed. If the horse reaches this level through the harmonious development of his physique and mental abilities so that he "gives the impression of doing of his own accord what is required of him", the trainer certainly has done an excellent job.

At this point the horse is a pleasure to ride. He is on the aids and thus ready for *special training*, which will allow the adult horse to excel in the discipline for which he has the most talent. Solid *basic training* is the best preparation for specialization in higher levels of dressage, eventing or jumping. This all-around work is the best way to ensure that a horse will be mentally and physically sound and willing to perform well into his older years.

One must always pay attention that it should be *the horse* who is doing the work. It must not be allowed that the rider puts in a lot of effort while the horse conserves itself.

The natural forward movement of the horse is a worthy possession that one cannot afford to sacrifice. When that gets lost, look for the cause. It often lies in insufficient well-being or expecting too much too soon.

Whenever one sees a horse perform unwillingly, with tension and resistance, one can be quite sure it is because of a lack of proper *basic training*. Such horses cannot move freely, lightly or balanced like they could before they entered training because of stiffness, crookedness and pain. They have been forced to work on levels for which they actually weren't ready. Unfortunately, we see quite a few riders presenting themselves this way at shows, especially at the higher levels, perhaps hoping for a kind judge. Their horses have been drilled in higher level movements, but in doing so have also lost their natural freedom, lightness and brilliance. Such presentations are ridiculous and most certainly have nothing in common with classical dressage!

Bad pictures in jumping also result from bad *basic training* on the flat. Horses not properly "on the aids", unbalanced, and stiff do not allow the rider to present himself in an attractive manner.

The only way to correct this is by returning to lower-level requirements, to re-establish regularity, balance and suppleness, elements of the *basic training*, the essentials that must dominate to achieve any kind of harmony between horse and rider.

In my opinion the only way to avoid this deviation from the classical principles is a qualification system as practised in Germany. This system would not allow a horse/rider pair to compete at a higher level until they have proven themselves successful at the previous level.

The basic rules of training have remained unchanged since the time of Xenophon. To touch them would be to wander onto dangerous territory.

Unfortunately, there are deviations in the practical handling of the pure art of training. These are for singular cases and should be seen as such. These ways should never be accepted as "new methods in training".

THE TRAINING TREE

*"A good rider with an average horse achieves more than
an average rider with a good horse."*

We know that basic training is an all-around prerequisite to the three equestrian disciplines: dressage, cross country, and jumping. This way, the young horse will develop at his best, mentally as well as physically. After two years in basic training, he can proceed to special training and excel in the discipline for which he has the most talent.

We also know that in basic training, in addition to the work on the flat, gymnastics with cavalletti and work over small fences can help develop muscles and elasticity. Both gymnastics and education are essentially what dressage is all about.

There are ten elements of education that dovetail with each other and are the keys to dressage. Everyone has heard of "Schwung", straightening, rhythm and relaxation. But how do they develop, and in which order? A good trainer knows how to put these elements together, both in groups and in a logical order.

For a better understanding take a look at the Training Tree (Fig. 6).

This image should give you an understanding of the progressive steps in your training. The trunk is composed of ten elements, which must be developed in sequence during the two years of basic training of the young horse. These elements, carefully built upon one another, create a solid tree trunk that can support a beautiful crown of branches.

The beauty of the crown is the result of special training, based on this solid, sound trunk.

Fig. 6

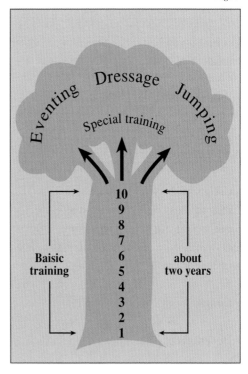

14

The fruits are a great jumper, a successful eventer, or a breathtaking dressage horse.

The ten elements of the Training tree are the following (in alphabetical order):

Balance
Collection
Contact
Durchlässigkeit (often translated as suppleness)
Freedom (of the gaits)
On the Aids
Regularity
Relaxation
Schwung (often translated as impulsion)
Straightness

In what sequence would you place these ten elements? For the correct answer, read on, but first try to find your own answer. First consider what each of these elements mean.

• **Balance** is the relative distribution of the weight of horse and rider upon the left and right reins (lateral balance) and the fore and hind legs (longitudinal balance).

• **Collection** is the state in which the horse is gathered together. The hindquarters carry more weight, the forehand becomes lighter, and the horse becomes more elevated in the withers and neck.

• **Contact** is the acceptance of the bit.

• **Durchlässigkeit**, a German term which is often translated as suppleness, though it is much more than looseness in the horse's body. **Durchlässigkeit** is the "quality in a horse that permits the aids (primarily the rein aids) to go through and reach and influence the hind legs". We can also consider the definition given for suppleness, which is "the physical ability of the horse to shift the point of equilibrium smoothly forwards and back as well as laterally without stiffness or resistance. Suppleness is manifested by the horse´s fluid response to the rider's restraining and positioning aids of the rein and to the driving aids of the leg and seat. Suppleness is best judged in transitions." (USDF Rule Book). Another definition reads: Suppleness is "pliability, showing ability to smoothly adjust the carriage (longitudinal) and the position or bend (lateral) without impairment of the flow of movement, or of the balance" (USDF **Glossary of Judging Terms**).

• **Freedom** of the gaits is the reach and scope and lack of constriction in the movement of the fore and hind limbs. A horse that has freedom of gaits exhibits a desire to move forwards with natural ease.

• **On the Aids** is the state of a horse that has learned to respond to the directions from the rider's seat, legs and hands.

• **Regularity** is the correctness of the gait, including purity, evenness and levelness.

• **Relaxation** is the absence of tension in the horse's body and mind.

• **Schwung** is another German term that is often translated as impulsion. **Schwung** is "the powerful thrust emanating from the hindquarters propelling the horse forward and traveling through an elastic swinging back and relaxed neck" (USDF *Glossary of Judging Terms*, 1990).

• **Straightness** is the opposite of crookedness. A crooked horse does not travel properly on one track and thus is not able to use the propulsive power of the hindquarters.

Horse people know that one must respect the nature of the horse at all times and that one is obliged to learn as much as possible about his physical and psychological peculiarities. The more we know about our partner, the easier it will be to create a co-operative relationship, which is indispensable for any effective training. We also know that in training, we cannot force anything without endangering the horse's health. With this in mind, let us return to the Training Tree, which has now been completed (Fig. 7). It illustrates the ten elements of the trunk of the tree in the correct order. These ten elements must be considered in our dressage work throughout the *basic training*.

Dressage is the most important part of this all-around training, since it holds the keys for the work on a solid foundation. The trunk of the tree shows all the elements of this work that in the end makes the horse relaxed, obedient, and as de la Guérnière put it, "pleasurable to ride".

What do we mean by the *correct order*?

Correct order means that there is a particular sequence in which each element exists closely with neighbouring elements – those that precede as well as those that follow. But as in nature, no cell can live on its own. The fulfilment of each element depends on its relationship with neighbouring elements. That's why we never work just on one element – we work on phases that cover the neighbouring elements.

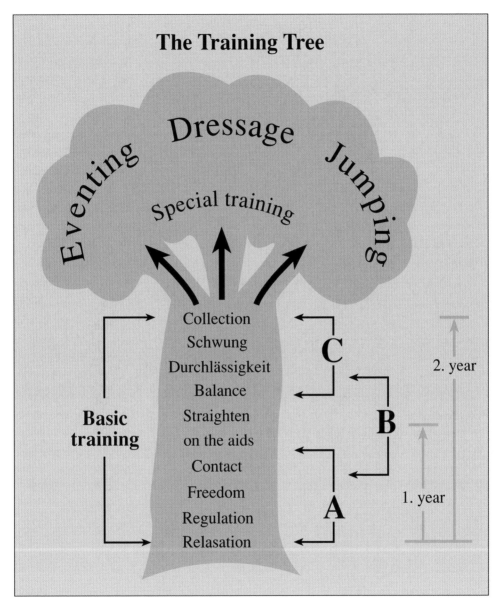

Fig. 7: The Training Tree
Phase A (on the way to training level) getting used to the rider´s weight, familiarizing with the aids and environment.
Phase B (on the way to First level) developing forward thrust.
Phase C (on the way to Second level) developing self-carriage.
The Training Tree concept offers basic training for all disciplines where suppleness and obedience are important.
It is the "lowest common denominator" for the often different ideas with regards to training and various methods of
training a horse pleasurable to ride.

Considering the interrelatedness of each element we see that there are three phases of basic training.

To achieve the criteria of **PHASE A** (on the way to Training Level), we mainly work on relaxation, regularity, freedom of the gaits and contact.

• **Relaxation** is the first element we must care for and establish. The relaxed horse is confident and able to learn.

• **Regularity** cannot be expected unless the horse is moving in a relaxed way, without tension in body or mind.

• **Freedom** of the gaits should not be asked for at the price of regularity.

• **Contact** can only be achieved by a relaxed horse that is moving regularly and freely forwards into the rein and accepting the bit.

To achieve the criteria of **PHASE B** (on the way to First Level), the horse that is on the aids now needs to work mainly on confirming contact and establishing straightness and balance.

• **Contact** (see above).

• **On the Aids** is a state that should be expected after the four elements of Phase A have been achieved.

• **Straightness** is the most important prerequisite for all further dressage training. It cannot be achieved without the horse being properly on the aids.

• **Balance** is the result of straightness.

To achieve the criteria of **PHASE C** (on the way to Second Level), we mainly work on balance, Durchlässigkeit, Schwung and collection.

• **Balance** (see above).

• **Durchlässigkeit** can best be proven in transitions. A badly balanced horse is not able to perform good transitions and is not pleasurable to ride. Without balance, there cannot be **Durchlässigkeit**. Without **Durchlässigkeit**, there cannot be **Schwung**.

• **Schwung** is thrust and spring in the steps, suppleness of the back, and engagement of the haunches. In order to achieve **Schwung**, the horse must be well balanced and **durchlässig** (supple).

• **Collection** means the horse is gathered together, has more carriage, elevation and more lightness. Collection cannot be achieved unless the other elements are properly established and confirmed. The capability to collect makes the horse ready to proceed to the higher levels of dressage.

Sounds logical, doesn´t it? It is, because all work is based on previous elements. The better each element is developed, the easier it will be to introduce the element that follows. The whole procedure corresponds to the natural abilities of the horse.

If you keep following these principles, you actually cannot do much wrong. If, however, you violate these principles, you will likely end up in disorder, faced with resistance and other problems.

Do you understand now why there are so many horses with problems? In almost all cases, one can be sure the problem is not with the horse but rather with the rider, who, for whatever reason, failed to follow the order given in the Training Tree.

Consider some examples:

• A rider has a hard time getting his horse "on the bit". The horse looks tense and unhappy.

Recommendation: Get the horse relaxed and ride him freely forwards on 20 meter circles before you ask for contact.

• A rider wants his horse to jump a fence. The horse leans to the left shoulder and runs out to the left.

Recommendation: The horse must be straightened out. The work on straightness, however, demands that the horse is properly on the aids.

• A rider wants his horse to lengthen strides in the trot. The horse is instead quickening the steps, running away. Obviously a tense or sore back.

Recommendation: Before the rider asks for lengthenings, he or she must make sure the horse is moving relaxed and regularly, accepting the bit, and maintaining steady contact. The rider must be able to make the horse chew the bit downwards and forwards so he can stretch his topline and start swinging in the back. The rider shouldn't ask for lengthening unless he or she can feel the waves of the swinging back. Lengthening strides means lengthening these waves by the seat and leg aids.

• The rider asks for the rein back and the horse resists, evading with the hindquarters.

Recommendation: The proper execution of the rein back depends on **Durchlässigkeit**. Only a supple and durchlässig horse will respond to half-halts. But **Durchlässigkeit** is based on balance and straightness. The rider must work on these elements first until the horse responds to half-halts. Once the horse knows how to half-halt, he will have no problem executing the rein back.

These four examples demonstrate some of the hundreds of "problems" you may meet on your way. If you ever get stuck with a problem, ask yourself what the reason is behind it, and always remain patient and fair. The Training Tree will help.

In most cases, the horse does not understand because of insufficient preparation. That´s why one must return to easier movements for re-establishing the horse´s confidence and co-operation. Afterwards, one may ask again for the movement, and in most cases the horse will respond as desired. That will be the time for reward and possibly also for quitting for the day.

If you ever decide to confront the horse, be sure to end up as a winner. After all is done, you must praise the horse for having done a good job. On the other hand, if you are not positive about the outcome of the confrontation, choose another course, with the insight that you have to learn a lot more about equitation.

The worst thing a rider can do is nag the horse. This is worth nothing. On the contrary, the horse becomes stubborn, the rider frustrated, and the process of teaching unnecessarily difficult.

Admittedly, following principles shown in the Training Tree for almost two years is a long way to go, but it is a steady and safe way. The horse, mentally and physically mature, will feel sound and happy – ready to perform whatever you ask of him.

Those who instead try shortcuts will only meet with a series of problems, wasting energy and time. In the long run, the course suggested here is always the shorter one.

Let's again take a look at the different phases in the TRAINING TREE. Within the two years of basic training, there are three phases of education.

PHASE A – The horse becomes accustomed to the rider's weight and offers co- operation (requirements for Training Level dressage tests).

PHASE B – Development of muscles, joints and tendons enables the horse to gradually propel himself forwards properly (requirements for First Level dressage tests).

PHASE C – The horse develops the capability for self-carriage and starts to perform all movements with lightness and ease (requirements for Second Level tests).

Like the ten elements, these three phases cannot be separated from one another. The transitions from one element to the next are fluid. The drawing shows which elements are expected to be established after one year of training. The horse should be able to perform a reasonable First Level test.

In the second year, the horse is on his way to Second Level with all the elements of the first year being confirmed, thus enabling the horse to win First Level tests. In general, one can say that the elements must be established as follows: within the first year elements one to five, within the second year elements six to ten.

The Training Tree, as we can see, gives us a clear idea of how to proceed in training a horse. We know that there are ten elements of education in basic training to be established in a certain order.

This order is absolutely indispensable for effective training, allowing for fluid transitions from one element to the next as the horse becomes consistently more and more confident and co-operative. He can thus give "the impression of doing of his own accord what is required of him".

The order of the elements in the Training Tree corresponds to the natural capabilities of the horse and should be applied in long-term training as well as daily sessions. By correct riding, it also preserves the horse's well-being.

A horse that has properly completed the programme of basic training and achieved its ten comprising elements is able to perform any Second Level test in an adequate manner. As a result, you should not worry about which Second Level test you enter. The only thing that matters is that your horse has mastered all the elements of the Training Tree.

If we follow the order of the Training Tree, we can expect each of its elements achieved to create further qualities as a bonus.

RELAXATION will create **calmness** and **confidence**.

REGULARITY will create **steadiness** pure rhythm and **tempo**.

FREEDOM will create **looseness** and a desire to move forwards.

CONTACT will create **connection** and an **acceptance** of the rider's hands.

ON THE AIDS will create **responsiveness**, **submissiveness** and **obedience**.

STRAIGHTNESS will create lateral **flexibility** and **propulsive power**.

BALANCE will create **lightness** and **ease**.

DURCHLÄSSIGKEIT will create **pliability**,a **forward-going** approach and **suppleness**.

SCHWUNG will create **energy, engagement, impulsion, liveliness** and **mobility**.

COLLECTION will create **elevation, cadence, suspension,** and **brilliance**.

As you can see, there are quite a lot of terms, which at first glance may be confusing, but the more one gets into the subject of training, the more familiar the terms will become, and the more comfortable you will become in using them.

The above composition of terms makes it easy to understand what, for instance, a horse on the aids should feel like, or what qualities a horse must have in order to be durchlässig. Here, in fact, all qualities prior to **Durchlässigkeit** must be visible and confirmed.

Now let us discuss each element we need to deal with in basic training. Our first element is relaxation.

RELAXATION
THE FIRST ELEMENT OF THE TRAINING TREE

"A good horse and a good rider are only so in mutual trust." (H. M. E)

The relaxed horse moves calmly forward without fear or pain. He is attentive to the rider, with no attempts to dash off or hurry. The rider is able to release and retake the reins at any gait without the horse altering pace, while the horse respects the low boards of an outdoor arena or the trail the rider wants to move on.

When relaxed, the horse does not show any tension anywhere in his body. He freely uses all his muscles throughout the body without resistance. Since the horse trusts his rider, he is confident and relaxed in his own mind.

I have seen many horses show irregularity in their gaits because they are not relaxed. This observation has led me to disagree with the German Training Scale, which places regularity prior to relaxation. In order for a horse to be regular, he must first be relaxed.

The horse´s eyes are calm and soft. The ears are not fixed – they play back and forth, demonstrating a confident awareness of both rider and environment. The mouth is closed and wet. The tongue is well placed under the bit. The horse is breathing normally after having sighed, high blowing several times. The neck is in a low position, thus helping the back muscles carry the rider´s weight.

The tail represents the last vertebrae of the spine. The way the horse carries the tail tells us a lot about his state of mind. Stiffness or crookedness indicates tension in the back. Swishing is generally a defence against a bad leg position of the rider. The relaxed horse carries the tail evenly and elastically, so it moves slightly in the rhythm of the walk and trot.

The time you must provide for the work on relaxation depends mainly on the nervous system of the horse and your riding skills. A calm horse won't give one much of a problem. A nervous horse, however, needs much time and patience. It is better to give a horse more time than miles.

Why does a horse get tense? As mentioned before, tension begins in the brain. The nervous system, which controls muscles all over the body, gets messages. If the horse gets messages signalling pain or danger, the horse becomes instantly tense and defensive.

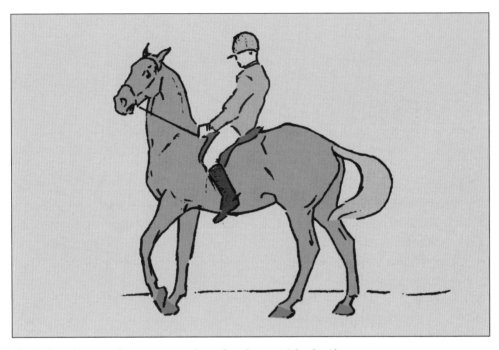

Fig. 8: Green horses tend to become tense due to the unknown weight of a rider.

Green horses that move in a relaxed and regular way on the lunge line often become tense as soon as riders mount them (Fig. 8).

The newness of the situation and the fact that he is not accustomed to having weight on his back makes the young horse suspicious and defensive. The back becomes tense, the horse holds his breath, and one false move in the saddle may put the rider in trouble. By bucking, the horse tries to get rid of the tension (or the rider).

Horses have a hard time learning how to balance the rider's weight in the different gaits, first on the flat, later in hilly country. An experienced and sensitive rider knows how to co-ordinate his or her body with the uncontrolled movements of the horse without pinching the legs. This enables the horse to handle the weight in a short time without getting tense.

There are other reasons a horse becomes tense. After an accident or severe stress the horse is in pain because the muscles spasm and fill up with lactic acid.

In natural healing, the brain gets a message from the part of the body that needs help and dispatches blood full of oxygen and nutrients to reduce the lactic acid. That, however, takes time to complete.

If the healing process is constantly being interrupted because the rider cannot wait until the horse is absolutely sound, the body builds blocks with muscle spasms, not allowing the messages to go through to the brain. In this case, no extra blood will be dispatched, and no further healing can be expected. Keep your eyes open and you will see many horses moving unevenly or stiffly for just this reason. They may be impaired in this way for the rest of their lives.

Sometimes horses become tense if the rider labours on movements that the horse cannot understand. In other words, the horse is not ready for these movements, and the rider has violated the principles of systematic training of the Training Tree.

Unfortunately, we still see horses in dressage shows competing at levels they are not ready for. Such stressed horses have obviously been forcefully drilled to show off with upper-level movements. But along the way they have lost all their natural character, charm and happiness.

Tension does not allow the horse to use his body as he would like to. If the horse´s back is tense, the rider cannot sit the trot. When bothered by a stiff and clumsy rider, the horse uses his flight instinct and defends himself by rushing. The walk is short, hasty and irregular. The canter is not round and does not show suspension (sometimes called "four-beat"). This kind of "dressage" is ridiculous and offensive to the dignity of the horse.

Let us say it again: Relaxation is the first element of the horse´s education and the very foundation for all further training. Keep your horse happy. Happy horses don´t get tense.

Before you start warming up, let your horse walk at least ten minutes with a loose rein. Give him a break whenever he deserves it. Stop serious work before the horse gets tired. Walk him after his work again for at least ten minutes to relax him.

Whenever possible, take your horse out for a recreational hack cross-country. If you are short on time, angry or nervous, don't start serious work. Take your horse out for a ride, relax and enjoy your friend.

Relaxation should be present in all movements and at all levels (Fig. 9).

How to achieve RELAXATION?

We know that tension comes from the horse being distracted, scared, in pain, or stressed for some reason. Permanent tension results in muscle problems that make the horse short-gaited, uneven, resistant and uncomfortable.

That´s why we must have a high esteem for relaxation, the most important element in basic training. Without relaxation, the horse cannot be receptive to the subtle influences of the rider.

The first serious work begins on the lunge line. How to lunge is beyond the scope of this book, but I would like to emphasize these points:

1) Lungeing is *work*, for the horse as well as the trainer. It demands the rider´s feel and concentration. Undisciplined running around is useless and can endanger the horse´s health.

2) Lungeing should be done in an area free of distractions.

Fig. 9: Even in piaffe, the highest grade of collection, the horse must be relaxed.
The author on "Wendischka" Hanoverian mare bred by himself.

3) Correct lungeing establishes and improves the relationship between you and your horse.

4) Your aids are lunge, whip and voice. Your commands should be determined and consistent so that the horse learns the meaning of the words.

5) Take your time. Relaxation is not fatigue or slackness. It starts in the horse´s mind with trust and confidence.

6) Lungeing begins and ends with an adequate period of walk.

For correct lungeing, you need a cavesson and side reins or draw reins long enough for the horse to stretch the neck forwards and downwards onto the bit.

After sufficient time working in the walk and trot, the normal horse will begin to relax, gradually loosening the muscles all over the body, nose slightly in front of the vertical, mouth about at the level of the point of the shoulder. Horses that don´t become relaxed in this way, for mental or physical reasons,

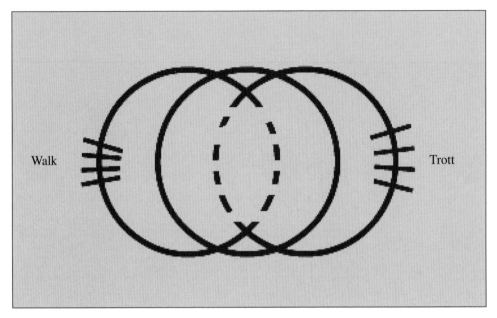

Walk   Trott

Fig. 10

need special treatment. Double lungeing, poles and cavalletti for walk and trot work, and a lot of patience can be useful tools for overcoming difficulties in this phase.

Work over cavalletti loosens the back muscles – first without a rider and later under the rider (Figs. 11, 12).

Under no circumstances should the horse be allowed to accelerate the pace or quicken the steps while going over the poles or cavalletti.

Make sure that the horse finds his natural tempo in which he is most comfortable. This is the best way he can find his balance and develop the desired muscles. Respecting your forward driving aids (whip and voice), he should maintain a permanent contact to your hand. All your aids should be given in a spirit of gentle determination. The following pro-

cedure proves to be most useful: middle circle without cavalletti, right circle for work at trot, left circle for walk (Fig. 10).

The first mounting is always an adventure for both horse and rider. Make sure that it will be a pleasant one! I won´t go into the details of the first mounting, but will underscore some common necessities that will help in establishing relaxation in this first phase of training.

- The better the preparation, the fewer the problems
- Familiar environment
- Experienced rider
- Experienced person to assist
- An additional calm horse for company
- The better the first mounting, the fewer problems later on.

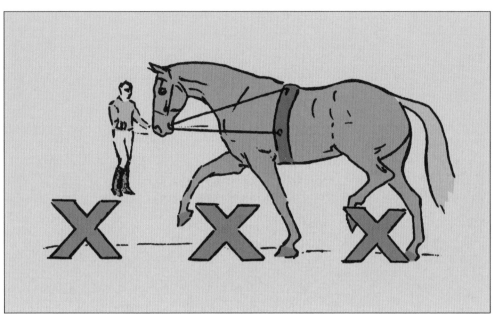

Fig. 11: Loosening work on the lunge to encourage relaxation.

Fig. 12: Loosening work to encourage relaxation under saddle in the forward seat.

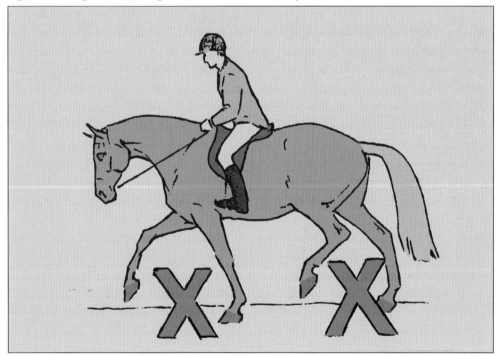

Fig. 13: Healthy, young horses enjoy free jumping.

How to carry a rider is the first serious learning process for the young horse. The young horse´s skeleton, muscles, tendons and ligaments are not built for carrying considerable additional weight. That is why at first, the horse stiffens the back and neck muscles and is very much handicapped in all his natural movements. Thus, the young horse must learn both carrying and balancing the rider without tension in all gaits. This takes time!

Under a lightweight, experienced rider, this process is likely to be problem-free. The elastic seat, feeling legs and independent hands will soon make the horse confident and relaxed. Unqualified riders can cause a lot of problems in your young horse.

Unfortunately many performance horses have never learned to use the back properly.

Without the proper functioning of this important bridge between the forehand and the hindquarters, the horse cannot perform at its maximum potential. Without a knowledgeable trainer to fix this, the horse will be handicapped for life.

Free jumping is a wonderful alternative to the daily routine. Horses enjoy these kinds of gymnastics, provided the procedure is done correctly. All my horses, including dressage prospects, love it. They get this treat during the winter months once a week (Fig. 13).

Unfortunately, some artificial aids actually inhibit rather than foster relaxation if not used properly. Draw reins and similar restrictive reins have come more and more into fashion. Carefully used for a limited time they can help overcome a back problem. In most cases, however, we see these draw reins used as a straightjacket. The horse is forced to move in a frame that is often not adequate to its conformation. The natural locomotion becomes restricted, and this encourages the horse to develop muscles of resistance. Once the back hurts, the horse is likely to find a way to somehow compensate for the pain. Experienced veterinarians know that many lower-limb problems originate from pain in the back.

When the back cannot relax and contribute to the horse´s movement as it should, the lower limbs usually try to compensate. In other words, to achieve a similar movement, the horse´s limbs must work harder and are therefore more prone to injury.

Rein lameness results from this kind of compensation. A horse with rein lameness has found a way to deal with an unbalanced rider who is stiff in one arm.

Now let us take a look at the body of the horse. There are two main muscle groups that play important roles: the upper one and the lower one (Figs. 14, 15).

Muscles function in two phases, by contracting and relaxing (and stretching). Contraction is the active phase that needs energy and consumes oxygen. In stretching, the muscle recovers and is supplied with new oxygen by blood circulation. If a muscle remains contracted for a longer period, it gets tense, as there is no recovery phase of stretching. This tension can build up and turn into painful cramping.

The young horse tightens the back muscles as soon as the rider gets on (Fig. 16). Since

Fig. 14: Top muskle groups

Fig. 15: Lower muskle groups

Fig. 16: Wrong! This horse has a tensed back. The top muscles are contracting while the lower ones are stretching.

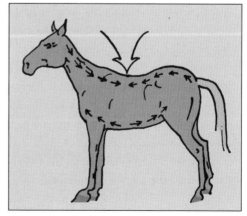

the back muscles are connected to the neck muscles as well as to the muscles of the croup, the neck is pulled up and the haunches are pulled back. The whole horse is affected by this tension, unable to breathe and move normally. He will tire quickly. The good rider respects this problem by just riding for short periods and allowing the young horse to rest and relax again and again.

No doubt, getting the back muscles to function is the most important aspect of basic training. The back must carry the rider and connect the forehand with the hindquarters. When the back does not function properly, it causes stiffness through the body, stiff haunches, tension in the neck, a blocked poll, and a "bad" mouth. Therefore, the relaxed back is indispensable for all further training.

Before the rider gets on, the young horse must settle down on the lunge line. He should stretch the head forwards and downwards, thus displaying a round topline with an elastic, swinging, back.

The unaccustomed weight of the rider makes the young horse contract the back and neck muscles, which in most cases affects his natural way of moving significantly. Regaining his relaxation and establishing his natural gaits under the new burden (Fig. 17) is the most challenging task of the rider during the first months of *basic training* (Phase A).

This process cannot be pushed. How much time it takes depends on the horse´s conformation as well as on the skill of the rider. Only the relaxed horse that works in harmony with the rider will develop the right mus-

cles in the right place. In this phase of training, we do not ride in the classical position, or the full seat. We use the forward seat for minimizing the burden of our weight. We do not ride in sitting trot unless the horse is on the bit, rounds his topline, and allows us to take a seat.

Once your horse is able to use his back and neck the way he should, he is ready for further training. The horse is not tense anymore and has re-established his natural way of moving. The steps can become regular and the horse will find the first contact with your hands. Moving freely forwards from your legs, he will gradually maintain a permanent contact with your light hands. He will learn to listen to your aids, confirming a clear rhythm and a steady tempo.

In further training you might use cavalletti in all gaits, work uphill and downhill, ride movements like turns and circles on one track, or use leg yielding. These exercises develop the muscles your horse will need in the future. They are gymnastics for improving elasticity and skill. This makes the horse relaxed and confident for further co-operation.

A highly recommended exercise for loosening the back and neck muscles is asking the horse *"to chew the bit out of the hand"* on a 20-metre circle. It invites the horse to "give" in the upper muscle group and should be applied as a reward for a good performance. It is extremely useful for making the horse stretch onto the bit while rounding the topline, thus demonstrating confidence as well as a sound back.

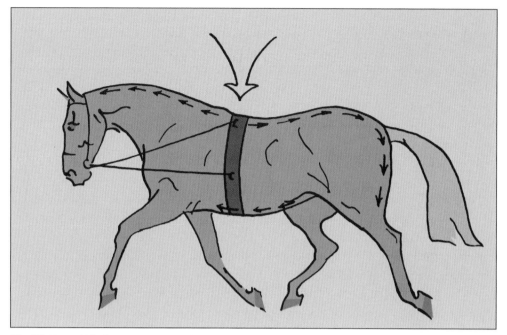

Fig. 17: Correct! The horse relaxes its back, the top muscles stretch while the lower muscles contract.

Horses of all levels (even Grand Prix), must be able to do this basic exercise sufficiently in walk, trot and canter. If a horse is not able to do this, he displays a severe lack of basic training. A horse that cannot chew the bit out of the hand does not use the back properly and is a **Schenkelgänger**, a "leg-goer", which is absolutely not desirable in dressage. Good judges know how to evaluate it.

If a horse remains suspicious and in permanent tension, the reason is most likely the rider. Anxious riders should not train such horses because they fail to inspire the horse´s confidence. The horses become uncertain and spooky, so after a while, everywhere they see bears in the trees.

This usually leads to the horse resisting moving forwards by backing or rearing up – a serious problem.

Green horses should be trained by riders who are not afraid and know how to convince the horse that there is no other way but forwards. After a while, the horse will agree. Horses respect authority.

The Warm-up: Preparation for Performance

A horse that is ready to begin work needs a certain time for warming up muscles and joints in order to relax mentally and physi-

Fig. 18: Overflexion of the head – to loosen the back muscles – seldom reaches the desired result in the long run, most of the time you lose the natural freshness and the freedom of gaits.

cally throughout the body. In the daily warm-up as well as in preparation for a test, you should follow the rules of the Training Tree. Starting with the elements of Phase A, you proceed to Phase B, and if necessary, to Phase C. The warm-up should be a tuning of the elements rather than work, much like the violinist tunes the instrument before demonstrating his or her art.

Your first goal is the swinging back, the regularity and the freedom of the gaits. Soon your horse will accept the bit and offer co-operation. Horses that have a hard time getting relaxed should be loosened up on the lunge line before the rider gets on.

Normally, at home, you know how to handle this, as you are not dependent on a time schedule. You can extend your warm-up as long as you need to get the horse relaxed and responsive. In competitions, however, there is a bell that calls you into the ring, so you must plan in advance and provide enough time for your horse to get ready to compete. But how much time is "enough time"? That depends on the horse´s temperament, his character, his state of training, as well as the atmosphere of the show grounds.

The warm-up for a dressage test can vary from 15 minutes to up to two hours or more. The goal is *not* to drill movements of the test again and again. It is the mental and physical relaxation that matters, because only a relaxed horse will listen to the aids and concentrate in the ring. No trainer of any other sport would ask for serious work or effort during the warm-up.

In general, I like to say that the warm-up is more a matter of time rather than of miles. A horse that has been chased around the warm-up ring for ten miles or more may be tired, but not relaxed and ready to compete.

Unfortunately, in our competitions, we still see quite a few riders in the warm-up area drilling the movements of the test or labouring on movements for which the horse has not even a foundation!

As a consequence, the horse enters the ring tense and sour, moving around unevenly and spiritlessly.

Event riders sometimes take hours to get their horses relaxed and ready for the test. A high-spirited event horse in top condition may need three hours to get relaxed enough in body and mind. Such a horse can be calmed by being kept busy with simple things, not necessarily riding. These things, like unloading and loading on the trailer, walking the grounds, riding for short periods, can be repeated again and again in order to distract the horse from the show atmosphere.

Sometimes successful riders warm up their horses by overflexing them in an extremely round frame. This exercise requires some explanation. If it is executed excessively or incorrectly it can do great damage. If it is done correctly it can be useful. The horse´s back connects the quarters with the forehand like a bridge. Under the rider´s weight, this bridge cannot function unless the back muscles are strong enough and work without tension. To make sure that the horse enters the ring relaxed and submissive, it *can* be useful to overflex the horse´s neck for a limited time in order to achieve relaxation by a maximum stretching of the topline (Fig. 18).

This way, poor back muscles can be strengthened, or strong and tight ones can be loosened up. Highly strung horses will get bored with the monotony of the work and calm down, since there is nothing to see but the ground.

To overflex properly, however, requires a sensitive and effective rider who knows how to keep the horse connected. As long as the rider is able to elevate the forehand (the poll being the highest point), and to create engagement, as well as impulsion from the haunches at any time, it is not a violation of the principles of classical dressage.

But there are some warnings:

1. First, this method should not be practised by riders who do not know how to mobilize the haunches to keep the horse connected from behind and how to elevate the forehand at any time.

2. Secondly, inexperienced riders will end up with problems such as a horse that is behind the bit, dead in the back, on the forehand, and restricted in the gaits, without engagement, and resistant. Unfortunately, this is quite a common occurence.

3. Thirdly, keeping the horse permanently overflexed ruins his natural flair and has nothing to do with classical dressage.

Finally, young horses that do not use the back properly need to be ridden "long and low" so that they can develop the muscles necessary for a Training Level frame. Once, however, the horse carries the rider without a problem, maintaining contact with his hands, it would be incorrect to continue riding in this way. We do not want the horse unnecessarily on the forehand.

Once the horse has developed so that it can carry the rider, the time has come to ask the horse for more engagement from behind, resulting in some elevation in the front.

REGULARITY
THE SECOND ELEMENT OF THE TRAINING TREE

"The fanciest movement means nothing once the gait is not regular."

The horse must move evenly and regularly. This fundamental feature one must have in mind when training a horse, in any gait and at whatever level. No dressage test can be satisfactory unless the horse is moving relaxed and regularly. Even the perfect execution of a movement cannot be scored sufficient once there is a slight irregularity in the correctness of the gait.

That´s why "purity of the gaits", which means regularity and evenness, is regarded as the most important feature of the Collective Marks of the FEI dressage tests.

The USDF *Glossary of Judging Terms* puts it like this: "Regularity refers to the correctness of the gait, including purity, evenness, and levelness. Irregularities may be momentary or pervasive; they may or may not be caused by unsoundness. In the Collective Marks for gaits regularity is used to address only purity and soundness – not unvarying tempo."

At this point it may be helpful to clarify the meaning of some aspects involved in regularity that are sometimes mistakenly used. The definitions are taken partly from the above-mentioned *Glossary of Judging Terms*.

Gait: For dressage purposes there are three gaits – walk, trot and canter.

Beat: Footfalls within a gait. A hoof (or pair of hooves simultaneously) striking the ground.

Pace: Any of the variations within each gait: collected, working, lengthened, medium, extended. The variations of the paces are correlated with strides per mile.

Stride: The cycle of movements that is completed when the horse´s legs regain their initial positions. At the trot, for example, it would include a beat (footfall of one diagonal pair), a period of suspension, another beat, and another period of suspension. The length of stride refers to the amount of ground covered by the above entire sequence.

Rhythm: The characteristic sequence of footfalls and phases of a given gait. In dressage, the only correct rhythms are those of the pure walk (four-beat rhythm), the pure trot (two-beat rhythm), and pure canter (three- beat rhythm). Do not confuse rhythm with tempo.

Rhythm must be regular at all times. Any deviation from the pure rhythm tells us there is a problem. If you find out that the horse is lame or sore for some reason, consult a veterinarian. There are horses that show a pure rhythm while moving freely but become uneven under a rider. In most cases, the reason for this tension in the horse results from fear, pain, or just plain unhappiness. A sensitive rider can solve such a problem.

Do not confuse rhythm or tempo with cadence. Cadence is a marked accent of the rhythm with elasticity and is an outcome of collection (the last element of the Training Tree) and elevation.

Tempo: The rate of repetition of the rhythm – the frequency of strides or beats per minute. The frequency of the footfalls at a given gait should not alter, no matter at what pace the horse is moving. Tempo is not necessarily correlated with the length of strides or speed.

Each horse has its own natural tempo he feels happy about (compare a pony to a normal-sized horse). This tempo must be stabilized in the daily sessions. A steady tempo gives the rider an excellent opportunity to control the timing of the aids and co-ordinate them with the horse´s motion – a prerequisite for invisible aids and harmony. Freestyle competitors use the metronome to find music that is suitable to the specific natural tempo of their horses.

When in transitions, the horse is changing the pace (lengthening or shortening strides). The strides must remain steady both in rhythm and in tempo.

Speed: The miles per hour at which the horse is moving. Speed should not be mistaken for tempo. The horse increases speed by making a transition either to another gait (trot to canter, for example), or to another pace (lengthening strides). Increasing the speed by quickening the tempo is a severe fault in dressage!

The rider is always striving for pure rhythm and steady tempo. Provided the gaits are regular, and provided the rider does not interfere with the natural movement of the horse, there should be no problem. However, the purity of the rhythm depends a great deal on the rider's seat and aids, and consequently, on feel. A rider who is not elastic, not balanced, and is not able to feel, interferes considerably with the regular movement of the horse.

That is why the independent, dynamic seat (I hate the term correct seat) is indispensable for any successful training of a horse. That is also why young prospects should not be trained by clumsy riders.

Riders who, for whatever reason, cannot follow the motion of the horse, do not feel a deviation in the rhythm or tempo and thus are not able to fix it. It is useless to yell at them asking for more engagement – they just cannot do this. That is why wise instructors spend their time primarily on improving the seat and the feel of their students on well-trained horses. A good seat is a lifelong investment. It is a possession that cannot be lost.

The Three Gaits

Now let us look at the three gaits, that is the rhythm of the walk, trot and canter. To better understand the footfall sequence, we have

Fig. 19

numbered the four feet: left hind is 1, left front is 2, right hind is 3, and right front is 4 (Fig. 19). In the graphics below, the circles above the numbers stand for the footfalls on the ground. (I think it is important to start counting with a hind foot, because the drive comes from there and plays an extensive role in the leg aids).

The **walk** is a four-beat movement. Listen to the beats of the sound horse walking along at his natural tempo. The sequence of the footfalls is even, like clockwork. First, right hind; second, right front; third, left hind; fourth, left front.

Any deviation from this rhythm is reason for suspicion.

Tension under the rider can already provoke serious problems in the walk, like short steps, rein lameness, and pacing. Any attempt to flex the neck too early in training results in a shortening and paralysis of the steps.

Riders who work with the hands (especially on the hard side), rather than using the seat and legs to straighten the horse, end up causing rein lameness. The horse cannot be blamed, since it was the rider who taught him this. So it is the rider whose riding habits need straightening out first.

Pacing is a severe fault in the walk. The horse doesn´t move in a pure four-beat rhythm. The rhythm you hear is:

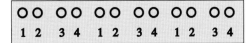

In the worst case, the horse is pacing almost like a camel, which sounds like this:

People who are not musical at all may not hear the difference. They should, however, see it.

In dressage, a good walk scores high. That is why when purchasing a dressage prospect, people look for an extreme overreach at the walk.

Without a doubt, such a walk is a present from heaven and should be handled like a treasure. However, there are, unfortunately, always riders and trainers who do not understand or care. They push the horses into a "dressage" frame for which the horse is neither mentally nor physically ready. For violating the principles of the Training Tree, people have to pay the price, in this case, the pacing of the horse.

Be careful in training horses with an extreme walk and large overreach. Do not ask for collected walk unless the horse is absolutely supple, remembering that *Durchlässigkeit* is the eighth element of the Training Tree.

Pacing is a bad habit and hard to fix. Once the horse starts pacing, return to loosening work on a long rein, go hacking in the country, and use cavalletti for the walk. Work on the slope and leg-yielding, correctly executed, are excellent exercises for re-establishing a pure walk rhythm. This is the only way to get rid of the tension, which is the cause of the problem.

Horses that nature did not favour with a good walk cannot be helped very much. Lots of gymnastics on a long rein can help, once the rider feels the sequence of the steps and knows how to adjust the aids to the motion of the horse. This is a prerequisite for improving any gait.

The **trot** is a two-beat movement. When correct, the two diagonals step with absolute regularity in a pure rhythm. Irregularities usually result from tension, just as in the walk. In addition, tension can cause a passage-like movement which, as an evasion from the pure trot, should not be tolerated.

The footfalls of the trot sound like this:

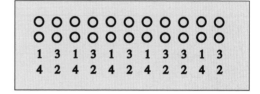

Horses with a short trot do not swing in the back due to bad training. Remember, that the first element in the Training Tree is relaxation!

The **canter** is a three-beat movement. You hear the beats of the right lead canter like this:

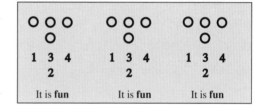

Notice the phase of suspension and the emphasis on fun.

As in the walk and trot, tension can cause irregularities in the canter. The most common fault is the so-called "four-beat" canter, which on the right lead in its extreme execution sounds like this:

In the four-beat canter, the diagonal feet (3 and 2) are not stepping simultaneously. In addition, the phase of suspension is almost not perceptible.

Fig. 20: Once in a while the dressage prospect also needs a real gallop. (Photo: Alan Lang)

The canter strides are not jumps anymore. No horse is born with a four-beat canter. This bad habit results from a lack of impulsion and liveliness. Obviously, the rider is not able to create impulsion and mistakes a shortening of the pace for collection. Violating the order of the Training Tree, the rider inadvertently teaches the collected canter without **Schwung** and suspension, and ends up with a four-beat canter. Remember, you cannot have collection without Schwung – Element 10 (collection) comes after Element 9 (**Schwung**). To re-establish a pure rhythm, the rider must first stop attempts to ride "collected". The rider must ride a lively working canter in an adequate frame. Once the rhythm is achieved, the rider may include transitions between working and medium canter. A new attempt at collected canter should not be made unless the rider has learned (on a lazy horse) how to create impulsion.

To be conclude, the gallop should be mentioned. In this high-speed canter, with an optimum moment of suspension, the front feet reach extremely far forwards so that the footfalls of the diagonal feet 3 and 2 cannot be simultaneous anymore.

FREEDOM
THE THIRD ELEMENT OF
THE TRAINING TREE

"In riding a horse we borrow freedom." (Helene Thomson)

Before asking for contact, we must be sure that the horse is able to carry the rider´s weight without tension and that there are no restrictions to the natural way the horse is moving. The gaits must be relaxed, regular and free.

Freedom of the gaits is the third element of the Training Tree, following relaxation and regularity. It refers to the lack of constriction of the joints of the horse´s legs, including the shoulders and hips, and the reach and scope in the movement.

Freedom of the gaits is closely related to the "desire to move forwards", which is also an important feature of the Collective Marks in FEI tests.

Rushing at the walk, trot or canter should not be mistaken for freedom. Horses rush when they are afraid, in pain, or simply uncomfortable. In these cases, the rider must return to working on the previous elements again, since the horse cannot move with freedom unless relaxation and regularity (Elements 1 and 2) are confirmed.

Sports therapist Jack Meagher regards *freedom* and *ease of motion* to be the most basic physiological requirement of muscles. "A lot of horses are performing below their capabilities not because they are lame or have any structural deformity, but because of miserable training they have lost the synchronized flow of motion required. Those horses need nothing more than a good rider or a knowledgeable therapist who will free up the restricted areas."

In fact, correct training is physically therapeutic, since "this noble art" of dressage "is solely to make the horse supple, relaxed, flexible, compliant and obedient", as de la Guérnière wrote.

Unfortunately, we see quite a few riders violating the rules of the Training Tree. They start working on contact (Element 4) before the gaits are free (Element 3). They don´t ride forwards from the active haunches into passive hands. They ride backwards from the active hands to the passive haunches. This is a severe fault that ruins the natural gaits, resulting in general constriction, a pacing walk, a rushing trot – or sometimes a four-beat canter!

Using draw reins without effective aids from seat and legs is like putting a straightjacket on the horse – it restricts *the freedom of the gaits* remarkably. No serious trainer will allow a student to replace a lack of riding capability by using draw reins.

Relaxation, regularity and freedom build the foundation for the work on *contact*. These four elements are the main building blocks in Phase A of the Training Tree. The confirmation of the elements in Phase A is what we need for re-establishing the natural gaits under the addition of a rider´s weight and for proceeding on to Training Level. Any attempts to perform fancy movements at the price of these basic elements will end up damaging the flair of the horse and will lead to further problems in later training.

Unfortunately, these days there are many trainers practising this kind of "dressage". Judges must not tolerate these presentations. They carry the responsibility for the preservation of the purity of "this noble art" and must seriously penalize any deviations from the classical rules.

CONTACT
THE FOURTH ELEMENT OF
THE TRAINING TREE

"There is no communication without contact."

The USDF **Glossary of Judging Terms** defines contact as "Tautness or stretch of the reins. Correct contact or acceptance of contact is determined by the elasticity of the connection between horse and rider." Unfortunately, aspects of this definition are misleading. Tautness means "pulled" or "drawn tight", which is not desirable at all.

The relaxed and regularly moving youngster will stretch his neck and round his topline. Encouraged by the rider´s legs, he will soon seek the offered hand. Before long, the horse will accept the bit and will find the first contact. At this point, the reins are slightly stretched. By following the nodding motion of the neck, the rider develops the feeling of his hands being connected with the horse´s mouth, since there is no tension in the muscles throughout the neck, poll´ and jaws. The nose is slightly in front of the vertical, the mouth is supple, the lips are closed, and the tongue is well placed under the bit. The glands produce the saliva necessary to keep the mouth wet and sensitive.

Maintaining this permanent, gentle connection, the rider will give his horse the chance to start the first communication. What a great feeling it is when the green horse first attempts to communicate! The horse indicates readiness for co-operation, the prerequisite for any successful training. Take it as a gift!

This state should be achieved within the first weeks of training, as well as later on in the daily training sessions to come. It is an indispensable part of the warm-up, no matter what the level.

The horse, being comfortable with the soft and steady hands, has achieved longitudinal flexibility. He is accepting the bit and will maintain contact of his own accord. The horse is coming on the bit. However, he is not yet on the aids.

Riders sometimes have a hard time maintaining a light contact. It takes quite a while before they learn to follow with the hands. The hands should be thought of as part of the horse´s mouth, and thus independent from the motion of the rider´s body. Good hands depend on a good seat. It would be useless to remind a student again and again to keep his hands quiet as long as he cannot sit quietly.

The correct position of the hands (they must be vertical so that when opened the palms are visible) is a prerequisite for a supple, feeling hand that follows the motion of the horse´s mouth. I like the image Sally Swift gives in her book **Centered Riding**, of holding two small birds in each hand without hurting them or letting them get away.

At no time are the hands the ones to create contact. This is a common fault. They are just reacting to the asking aids from the seat and legs, as we are working the entire horse, not only the neck. The relaxed and freely moving horse that is giving in the back will give in its poll and jaw and will accept the invitation of reins offered. This way, the desired position of the neck comes as a result of keeping the order of the Training Tree.

Green horses travel more or less crookedly. That´s why they often accept one rein more than the other. In most cases, they drop the left shoulder and lean on the left rein. Quite often, we see riders jerking on that left rein trying to straighten the horse, which results in the tilting of the horse´s head and the body becoming S-shaped.

At this stage of training, we shouldn´t worry about getting the horse straight. Rather we should care at first about the contact being the same on both reins – no matter where the horse´s head is pointing. At this point we are also concerned with the introduction of the meaning of the aids by seat and legs.

Later on, the horse must learn to bend throughout the body in order to stay on one track at all times. This way only, the thrust from the hind feet can travel throughout the horse. The first connection between the hind feet and hands is achieved, and the rider gets

the sensation of feeling the right hind foot in the right hand and the left hind foot in the left hand. To get there, we patiently teach the horse to understand the signals from the seat, legs and hands within the first year of training. In this way, the horse will learn to be on the aids and ready for the important work on straightness. The quality of contact will improve with the development of straightness. The more consistently the horse travels on one track, the more the rider will feel the thrust of the hind feet in his hands. In other words, the better the straightness, the better the contact.

Once the horse is on the aids, a good way to check the quality of the contact is by pushing the reins gently forward and downward some steps or strides, while supporting well with the seat and legs.

Fig. 21: Correct! The horse relaxes forwards-downwards as a reward.

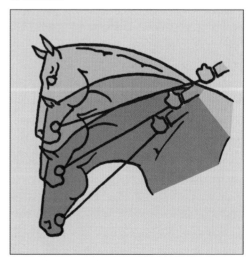

Fig. 22: Wrong! The horse stretches its neck without contact or connection to the backhand, this way the back does not round. The "Bridge" between forehand and hindquarters breaks in two.

Like being pushed by two sticks, the neck stretches in the desired way, with the mouth maintaining the contact. The horse remains *on the bit*, taking the stretching as a reward, and relaxes (Fig. 21).

In this exercise, which is practised at the famous German Cavalry School in Hanover, the horse learns to round the topline (especially at the canter).

This is also profitable for later training over fences and developing the bascule. Unfortunately in today´s jumping competitions one sees quite a lot of horses that certainly have not been trained in this way.

It is also a good way for teaching the horse to chew the reins out of the hands, a basic exercise of great value! If the horse does not follow the hands forwards and downwards while maintaining contact, one can be sure that there is something wrong about the relaxation of the back. In this case, the rider must show him the way to the ground, a very helpful exercise on a 20-metre circle. Riders who are not able to push a horse through may use draw reins for a limited time. A good rider does not need that tool.

As mentioned before, making the horse chew the reins out of the hand is an exercise of great value. Riders who do not have enough driving capacity from their aids cannot keep the horse connected from behind. Instead of making the horse stretch the correct way in order to loosen the back muscles, they just let the reins go. In consequence, the horse pulls the reins out of the hand, sticking the nose out. Tense all over the body, the horse rushes away with quick, uneven steps and cannot find the rhythm (Fig. 22).

Whenever the young horse has worked a certain amount of time in the desired contact, you should give him a break. Let him chew the reins out of the hand, give him a pat, and ask for a free walk with a loose rein. The horse´s muscles can recover and the horse remains willing for further work.

Due to poor riding the horse may be:

- Above the bit
- Behind the bit
- Fighting the hand
- Tossing the head
- Leaning on the rein
- Keeping the mouth open
- Tilting in the neck
- Accepting just one rein
- Grinding the teeth
- Pulling the tongue up
- Stretching the tongue out
- Putting the tongue over the bit

All of these undesirable behaviours indicate a lack of co-operation and attempts to evade contact. But do not let us blame the horse for a "bad mouth", a "stiff poll", or other bad habits. Let us rather have the insight that all these behaviours are reactions to poor riding and training. They are the only way the horse can tell the rider about the rider´s bad habits and what is wrong with the riding.

In most cases, the reason lies in the hand that bothers the horse. But as we know, there cannot be a good hand without a good seat, which enables the rider to use the legs efficiently. This again is a prerequisite for good contact between rider and horse.

That is why the qualified trainer works primarily on the student´s seat and legs *before* allowing the student to ask for contact.

ON THE AIDS
THE FIFTH ELEMENT OF
THE TRAINING TREE

"Your aids should help the horse express himself."

By the end of the first year, the horse has accomplished Phase A of basic training and should be on the aids. The horse now is mentally and physically submissive. He "responds instantly and generously to all the aids, accepting contact and maintaining connection" (USDF *Glossary of Judging Terms*). Simply put, the horse is on the seat, on the legs, and on the bit. Wilhelm Müseler published a picture of a horse on the aids in his famous book, *Riding Logic* (Fig. 23).

The quality of being on the aids cannot be evaluated from a picture, since a picture shows the horse and rider at one particular moment in time. It can only be evaluated by observing the pair in action, as it is the voluntary submission of the horse that moves in a relaxed way, regularly, and freely in full harmony with the rider.

Before we discuss details, it should be said that the horse must learn to understand the meaning of the different aids. Only then will the horse respond, provided that he is able to respond. Effective aids are only those that are co-ordinated with the horse´s motion. The ability to feel the motion and to apply the seat, leg, and hand aids almost invisibly and in correct timing is called "the rider's tact".

Developing this sensitivity is the most challenging task of a good instructor.

Fig. 23: A Horse on the aids - such a picture does not exist. It is just:

*Full harmony between
horse and rider*

Now, what does it mean to be on the seat, on the legs, and on the bit? Let us discuss these three aspects of being on the aids.

On the Seat

A horse on the seat responds instantly and generously to the aids from the seat. To do so, the horse depends on a good classical dressage seat that enables the rider to co-ordinate his or her body with the horse´s movement in every situation. I don´t like to use the term "correct seat" because it implies stiffness. The dressage seat is balanced and dynamic, without tension or stiffness, and allows the rider to stick in the saddle and to feel and follow the waves of the elastically swinging back of the mount.

A seat without tension should not be mistaken for a seat that wobbles. The rider must sit relaxed but controlled and firm throughout the body. The seat is the key to sensitive riding that connects legs and hands for clear communication and effective aids.

The well-trained horse is a *Rückengänger* (a "back-goer"). "A horse whose back swings elastically with his gait, particularly at the trot", is thus capable of developing **Schwung** (impulsion).

The opposite is the absolutely undesirable **Schenkelgänger** (a leg-goer), "whose back does not swing or appear to participate in the horse´s movement" (USDF *Glossary of Judging Terms*). This horse is not on the seat, that is, the rider cannot expect a response when asking for more engagement. Quite a few horses are *Schenkelgänger* because they have never been taught to use the back. It takes a good rider to correct this.

The beginner rider needs a *Rückengänger* that moves balanced and steadily, thus sending the waves from his swinging back. In a very slow and controlled trot, the rider will relax and discover how to connect his seat to the undulating motion. Once the rider knows how to balance his or her body without pinching the legs, he will soon be able to follow the waves at the working trot. But no one will ever learn to sit the trot on a horse with a tense back. Posting the trot would give relief to both horse and rider.

As mentioned before, I am not going to go into details about issues you can find in any equestrian literature. However, some things should be noted.

Normal breathing is part of a good seat. The head must not hang down but should be carried freely and upwards. The eyes do not fix on one spot (the horse´s ears) but take in the general view. Aids from the seat need the support from the legs.

The seat can be passive (just following the motion), or it can be engaged (asking the horse for a response from the haunches). This engagement can be very gentle, which is desirable, or more demanding if necessary.

The seat can be giving and a reward for a proper response, or it can be disciplining and answer a disobedience, such as bucking (a buck may cause a horse to hurt himself in the back and so should be discouraged).

Fig. 24: Lengthening the stride means lengthening the waves of the swinging back. Shown here are 5 steps at working trot (above), and lengthening of the strides (below). The horse is "on the seat", the tempo does not change.

The seat can influence the waves of the back considerably. In co-operation with the legs and hands, it is the key for lengthening strides and for all transitions. A horse that, due to faulty training, does not produce these waves in his back is likely to quicken his steps when asked to lengthen strides, which is a serious fault (Fig. 24).

In equestrian literature, there are numerous publications about the rider´s position. Many discuss the legs and hands but only a few

explain how to influence the horse from the seat. Obviously only a few writers have experienced the feel of a responsive back and the refinement of the aids once the horse is on the seat.

Sometimes at dressage competitions one can see riders performing higher-level movements who cannot sit the extended trot. The horse is tight in the back and not comfortable at all. There are no waves developed in the horse´s back and the extensions seem to be a torture for both rider and horse.

Schenkelgänger are unhappy and certain-ly not pleasurable to ride. At higher levels, a tight back demonstrates *a severe lack of basic training* and must be regarded as an offence against the principles of classical dressage. Good judges should know what to do.

The extended trot must be a highlight in the higher-level dressage test. After work-ing on collected movements, it is a *relief* for the horse to "fly" forward. The rider just needs to allow the horse to demonstrate his full capacity so that everybody can enjoy it – the horse, the rider, the judges and the crowd.

The prerequisite for an aid by the seat is the ability to follow the motion in all gaits while maintaining good co-ordination with the horse's centre of gravity, no matter whether the rider is using the dressage seat, forward seat, two-point seat, or jumping a fence.

The horse will notice any deviation from this feeling. Sensitive in the back, he will respond to any indication from the seat. Aged school horses accustomed to taking care of beginner riders often ignore these aids (that's why they survive), while green horses some-times get irritated. The good rider will fix these problems in a few minutes.

A rider who does not follow with the seat bothers the horse, since in addition to carry-ing the weight, the horse must drag the rider. That's why the passive seat, in order to fol-low the motion and avoid being dragged, actually needs a certain activity from the low-er back. The aid from the seat is invisible. Its efficiency does not come from moving the

Fig. 25: Here the seat of the rider is demonstrated on a barrel.

seat back and forth in the saddle (like mak-ing a frozen sleigh move). Nor does it come from leaning the upper body forwards or backwards, this being a rather common fault.

The effectiveness of the seat lies in the way the rider pushes his seat bones forwards and downwards, *without changing the base of his seat* (that is the triangle formed by the seat bones and the crotch), and while stretching his body vertically (head up and heels down).

Of all the efforts that have been made to explain the rider´s influence by the seat, only a few are useful. The best way to teach the engagement of the seat is with a stool, barrel, or a wooden box of adequate size that allows the student to sit in the rider´s position on his seat bones. The seat is opened, the heels heavy on the ground (Fig. 25).

Now let us take a look at the demonstration in Figure 26. Here the rider understands what she is supposed to do – she must tip the barrel. Everyone can do it without a problem and without being taught which muscles to use and in what way. The student will find out how to tip the barrel without any difficulty and without even thinking of which muscles to use. She is just tipping the barrel with her seat, unconsciously engaging the muscles necessary. Once the student finds out how to engage the seat to tip the barrel, she has the right idea for engaging the seat in the saddle. The student will also learn that tipping the barrel is not possible without a solid foundation from the legs, which will make her understand that engaging the seat includes the engagement of the legs.

By slight pressure of his fingertips, the trainer can make the student increase or decrease the engagement of her seat (tip the barrel), which is extremely helpful in fine-tuning the aids for a proper half-halt. There will be no mystery anymore about this most important aid, the key to sensitive riding.

Now let us forget the tiring discussions about which muscles need to be contracted or relaxed when "bracing the back" (a misleading translation in a famous German book on riding). For decades, this unfortunate advice has caused a lot of confusion, even damage, in the dressage world. Let us simply "tip the barrel" so we engage the seat the way it should be and we have the key for the most important aid: the half halt.

This exercise is particularly educational and teaches the student not to tip the pelvis backwards. This would make the student *sit behind the seat bones – a serious fault*, which however, is frequently seen even in so-called "good" riders.

The spine gets crooked and stiff, thus feelingless, and the knees tend to move up. In order to compensate for the bouncing of his or her body, the rider projects the neck forward and bobs the head. (Fig. 27)

The well-trained horse responds to the engagement of the seat with more activity

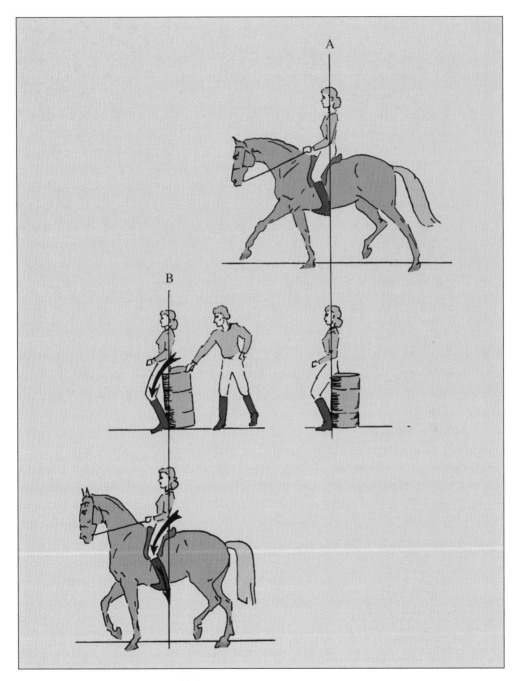

Fig. 26 Engaging the seat – key for half-halt
A The rider´s seat is connected to the swinging back of the horse at all times.
B When "tipping the barrel" the legs are placed so as to mobilize the hindquarters. The arrow shows the
direction of influence from the lower back down to the heels.

Fig. 27 Wrong, no engagement!
Shown here is the backwards tipped pelvis (a very common serious fault). The rider is "bracing the back" and sits behind the seatbones. This results in rounding of the rider´s back, loosening the effective position of the legs. This picture was taken at an international championship. Photo: J. Melissen

from behind, and the rider gets the feel of receiving this activity in the hands. This way, the seat becomes important in connecting and co-ordinating the aids at half-halts. The effectiveness of these aids depends on the function of the seat.

Once the rider knows how to engage the hindquarters by engaging the seat in the classical position, the rider will be able to do the same in the forward seat or in two-point. On the other hand, riders who have started out and kept riding in a forward seat have a hard time comprehending the engaging aids from the seat.

On the Legs

Recall that a horse on the aids is *on the seat, on the legs, and on the bit*. We know that the seat integrates the aids from the legs with those from the reins. The ability to follow the motion or to engage when necessary makes the seat the key for sensitive riding.

With the legs, the rider creates a circulation of energy throughout the horse that makes the horse move forwards onto the bit. The seat functions as a transmission between the *asking legs and the receiving hands*. Now let us discuss what it means for a horse to be *on the legs*. The horse is on the legs once it responds instantly and generously to the aids from the legs. Since all information to the horse starts from the rider´s lower leg, the leg aids are the most important, and the young horse should comprehend the meaning of those aids as soon as possible.

In the daily handling of the youngster, there are many possibilities to teach him to respond to a touch or to a light pressure by the fingers about three hands behind the elbow. When the young horse is tied to the stable, we can make him yield to one or the other side. On the lunge line, we use the whip to teach the young horse to move forwards or sideways.

When riding a young horse, one should always carry a short whip in order to teach him to listen to the leg. A forced use of the leg, like kicking in the ribs, is no aid; it is just bad horsemanship.

A tap with the whip just behind the calf will remind the horse to listen to the leg. The tap of the whip must come instantly and at the right moment and with appropriate strength so that the horse is impressed.

The whip itself should be fast – resistant, elastic, and not longer than 120 centimetres. Very long whips may be useful for a knowledgeable person helping from the ground. Being weak and sloppy, they are always late in the timing, so they irritate rather than help the horse. Sometimes at shows I think the longer the whip the poorer the rider.

On the other hand, the horse must be educated to go from the leg, not from the whip. The horse must be in front of the legs at all times, ready to go forwards, at the halt as well as the rein back.

Let me also address the use of spurs. The spur is *not* meant to drive the horse forwards! That is the job of the leg. The only reason to use the spur is to wake up a careless horse and make him listen to the leg. This action by the spur must be short but intensive so that the horse becomes convinced to willingly respond to an indication of the calf. This way, we educate the horse to be in front of the legs and to move on his own, demonstrating the desire to move forwards.

For example, if a horse ignores the aids for the canter depart, it would be wrong to urge him with the spurs, since he would most likely answer by just quickening the steps. In this case, he needs to be wakened up by an impressive kick from the spur that makes him listen and ready to go. Then, by an indication of an aid, the rider *allows* him to canter. Misusing the spur displays poor horsemanship.

Constant nagging with the spurs makes the horse insensitive and stubborn. Riders using physical effort to get the horse more lively often do not know how to adjust the leg aids to the foreward-thrusting motion of the hind feet. The horse cannot understand leg aids that are not co-ordinated with his motion. They are useless, and consequently, the rider gets exhausted after a few minutes of hard work. This certainly is not the way to train a horse! It must be the other way – the rider creates the design and the horse does the work.

Failures to teach a horse to move forwards from the legs may provoke serious problems.

Once the horse finds out how to hold back by ignoring the aids, he will before long end up resistant.

It is not physical strength that makes the horse co-operate with the rider. It is the amount of respect that the horse pays to a rider who convinces the horse with his skill. A skilled rider knows how to keep the horse on the aids, insists on accurate work and does not simply allow the horse to have his own way. A skilled rider also knows how much he or she can demand and uses rewards rather than discipline to be effective.

Extremely sensitive horses want to be hugged by the leg and need a very calm and firm leg. The horse must accept the leg before he can be asked to accept the bit.

Like the aids from the seat and from the reins, the leg aids must be adjusted to the horse´s motion. The only way the horse can understand and respond to a signal from the leg is when the corresponding hind foot is about to strike off the ground. A proper response from the spur or whip also cannot be expected unless this enforced aid fits the motion of the horse. We ride with the horse, not against the horse.

Concerning the timing of the aids in general, we can say that the right rein and right leg communicate with the right hind, and the left rein and the left leg communicate with the left hind of the horse. This sounds easy, but it requires quite a bit of practice to develop the feeling for correct timing.

Unfortunately, there are many riders who have never heard (or do not care) about ad-justing their aids to the motion of the horse. This skill is absolutely indispensable in classic equitation! Since they permanently ride against the horse, they use force and will never achieve the desired harmony. Most tensions, irregularities and disobedience occur simply for this reason. Sensitive riders, however, know how to co-ordinate the aids with the rhythm. They ride *with the horse* and can make him fly.

Since there are many riders using the legs improperly, there is a need for clarifying the priorities. First of all, from a deep seat, the legs hug the horse´s body in a calm and gentle way. The horse should feel safe and at home. It is like a father taking his child by the hand when things become frightening.

Secondly, in co-operation with the reins, the legs are providing the rails that keep the horse straight or bent on the track. Except when working on lateral movements, the horse should always be moving on one track – like a railway train. We will discuss this issue in connection with straightness, which is Element 6 of the Training Tree.

Thirdly, the legs provide the ignition for the hind feet, which function as the engine propelling the horse forwards. The well-trained horse moves forwards on his own, allowing the rider to use his legs for maintaining *straightness*, *tempo*, and *Schwung*. Good leg aids are almost invisible.

Prerequisite for correct leg aids is the proper position of the legs based on a well-balanced seat – whether it is the dressage seat, the forward seat, or the two-point seat. Since the leg is gently connected to the horse´s body (no more pressure than is necessary for holding a postcard between the calf of the leg and the horse´s belly), being steady and calm in all gaits, the horse will pay attention to a very little difference in pressure or position.

The leg position varies depending on what the rider asks of the horse.

Close to the girth, the leg pushes the horse forwards for engagement and for positioning or bending him from the inner side.

Close behind the girth (about one inch), the leg makes the horse yield from the inner side, like in leg-yielding or turns on the forehand.

One hand behind the girth, the leg acts as a counterpart to the inner leg. With more or less activity, it controls the hindquarters by preventing them from falling out.

Exaggerations in leg positions are just as ugly as conspicuous aids. The calmer the rider´s seat and legs, the more the horse will listen to a minimum of aids. When it is noisy, you must scream; when it is silent you can whisper.

Riding without stirrups is extremely necessary for developing a good seat. Every rider, whatever the level, should cross the irons once in a while to stretch the legs. However, for applying invisible aids on a well-balanced horse, you need stirrups, since a little increase in pressure from the foot on the iron should provoke a response from the horse. Prerequisite for this sophisticated aid is an elastic ankle and a sensitive but firm touch on the iron.

The length of the stirrup leathers depends on both the length of the rider´s legs and the volume of the horse´s body. The more body,

the longer the leathers. The main concern is the rider´s position in the saddle and the ability to hug the horse easily by the inside of the thigh, the knee and the calf. The foot shouldn´t be forced to be parallel to the horse´s body (an often seen bad habit), since it would stiffen the ankle and prevent the necessary feeling.

It is the way the thigh is placed on the saddle, with the kneecap pointing straight forwards, that brings the foot into the correct position.

A good way to teach the horse the leg aids is leg-yielding. Here we introduce the meaning of the inside and outside leg. This basic exercise is also extremely useful for training beginner riders to apply the legs correctly and to co-ordinate the timing of the aids with the motion of the horse. Later on, a turn on the forehand or even a turn on the haunches can be added. Both are excellent exercises to teach the meaning of the inside and outside leg to the green horse (by an experienced rider) and to the green rider (by an experienced horse).

Once the young horse executes these movements properly – relaxed, on the aids, straight, positioned and rhythmic – responding instantly, without tension or resistance to indications of the legs and reins, the trainer has done an excellent job.

Keeping the importance of being on the seat and on the leg in mind, we come to the meaning of being on the bit. This topic has been discussed in depth in the chapter on contact, Element 4 of the Training Tree, but let us review here a few of the important principles relating to it.

Fig. 28: Allowing the horse "to chew the bit out of the hand" – the connection to the horse's mouth stays.

On the Bit

A horse that is on the bit softly and quietly accepts contact with a stretched neck and with lateral and longitudinal flexion as required.

• Rein aids are almost invisible. Indications occur from a slightly closed hand and an elastic wrist by sponging and easing the fingers.

• "Giving" is not possible without having something to give.

• No "taking" without support from the legs.

• The reins can be supporting in order to keep the horse in the rails on straight and curved lines.

• Non-allowing reins may be necessary for pushing the horse through (by engaging the seat and legs), in order to make him yield at the poll, a prerequisite for rounding his topline.

• A soft rein is not a loose or slugging rein. The soft rein is always stretched, due to elastic joints of the arm (shoulder, elbow, wrist), and should look like two rods.

• Rein aids are given in co-operation with the legs and seat. They should never be dominating.

• The legs are asking. The hands are receiving and allowing.

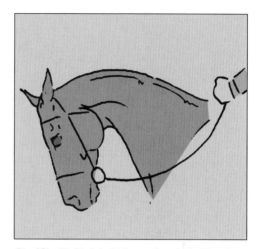

Fig. 29a: The horse is behind the vertical; however, the contact has remained. He is not "behind the bit".

Fig. 29b: "Behind the bit", a serious fault. There is no contact on the rein, due to a lack of activity from the hindquarters.

• Good rein aids are adjusted to the horse´s motion. The right rein follows and controls the right hind foot. The left rein does the same, co-operating with the left hind foot. This sounds logical, but it is not easy. It requires a lot of practice.

• All attempts to improve contact start from the seat and legs.

• The well-balanced horse does not need the reins as support.

• Reins in one hand (close above the withers) is an excellent way to check for honest contact (maintained by the horse) and lateral balance. When the horse keeps his rhythm and outline, the rider is on the correct road. When the horse escapes from the reins, the rider has to rebalance the horse.

• Asking the horse to chew the bit out of the hand is a highly recommended exercise for improving relaxation and contact. Within the first year of basic training, the horse should be taught to follow the forward and downward feeling hand in all three gaits, as if it were being *pushed* by two rods. This exercise was used by the German Cavalry School and has proven to be extremely helpful in keeping horses of all levels relaxed.

To summarize, we know that the horse *on the aids* is *on the seat, on the legs* and *on the bit*. Good aids are almost invisible. The prerequisite for good aids is a good seat. And finally, horses respect the knowledgeable and decisive rider who demands proper work and knows when to quit.

Invisible aids depend on perfect timing, since only aids given in this manner can be understood by the horse. This way any horse can be educated to respond sensitively to the aids.

Remember that it is easier to handle one pound of brain than a thousand pounds of muscle! And it is much easier to plant a new idea in the brain than to take an old one out.

For some horses, in order to get the back relaxed, it can be useful to ride them for a limited time slightly overbent in the neck, the nose slightly behind the vertical. As long as the horse is still accepting the bridle, it is not harmful (Fig. 29a).

A horse, however, that is sucking back in the neck, evading contact with the rider´s hand is not on the bit! It is behind the bit, which is a serious fault (Fig. 29b).

Whenever we have a problem with a horse not accepting the bit, we must think of the seat and legs. In most cases the seat is not balanced and the legs are not effective. A proper seat, however, is a prerequisite for a calm and sensitive hand that communicates with the horse´s mouth. Seat and leg aids always have priority over the reins. The hands are the receiving aids; they give rather than take. But one cannot give unless there is contact, and therefore something to give.

The proper seat that follows the motion is also indispensable for the proper use of the aids in their successive order – seat, leg, hands.

The process of getting the horse on the aids and submissive to the rider is not just a physical process, but a mental one as well. A horse that trusts his rider is submissive. The horse subordinates himself to the rider, who is the only one to make decisions. The horse understands the meaning of the aids when the horse has confidence in the rider. This takes time. Only the relaxed horse that moves regularly and freely will be mentally receptive to the invisible signals from the seat, legs and hands.

STRAIGHTNESS
THE SIXTH ELEMENT OF
THE TRAINING TREE

"Ride your horse forwards and straighten him." (Gustav Steinbrecht)

Towards the end of the first year of basic training, the young horse must be on the aids. The
horse has learned – more or less perfectly –
to respond to the aids from the seat, legs, and
hands, and should be able to perform a reasonable First Level test. He should also be
familiar with hacking cross-country, which
includes jumping small fences and ditches.

In this way, the mentally and physically
prepared young horse is ready to proceed to
Second Level. Unforeseen complications
notwithstanding, this should be achieved by
the end of the second year of training. By
then, the horse should be able to perform a
reasonable Second Level test and be successful in First Level.

The second year of basic training contains
fascinating elements to work on. Since the
horse is on the aids, we improve and confirm
the preceding elements in our daily sessions,
and we gradually include work on achieving
straightness.

I absolutely disagree with the German training scale that puts **Schwung** (9) prior to
straightness (6). After a lifetime of training
horses I am convinced that a horse must be

moving straight (in the rails) before one can
ask for **Schwung** (impulsion). I have seen too
many horses with problems just for this reason.

Everyone who drives a car knows that for
mechanical and safety reasons the car must
be "straightened" before it is allowed to leave
the repair shop.

Due to the co-operation of the legs and hands
– co-ordinated by the seat – we feel that there
is some connection between the hindquarters
and the mouth. This connection, however, cannot be perfect, since due to *natural crookedness*, the horse does not yet move straight.

There are enough theories and explanations
in equine literature about the natural crookedness in the horse, so we will not go into this
subject in detail. However, let me say that just
as most people are right-handed, most horses are right-footed. That is, the right hind is
stronger than the left. This quality is a gift
from nature that enables the horse in danger
to turn instantly (to the left) in flight. This
favours the capability of the body to bend to
the right more easily than to the left.

Crooked horses always have the possibility of ignoring the aids.

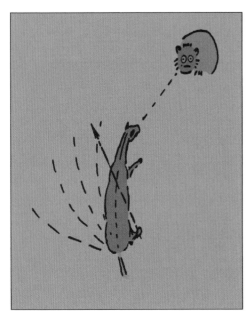

Fig. 30: The ghost in the bush...

Consider these examples:
• Most horses, since they are right-footed, tend to turn to the left once they see "bears in the trees". The right hind foot is the one that pushes the body away from the danger.
• Right-footed horses, when spooky, mostly watch out for (and find) "bears" at their right side. They use the crookedness for protection by bending the neck and body to the right, always ready to evade to the left. Those horses often do not care about the same things on their left side (the judge´s booth, flower arrangements along the dressage ring), because evading to the right is not as easy as evading to the left.
• In poor jumping, most disobedient horses run out to the left.

• Horses that insist on refusing to move forwards try to evade to the left and tend to rear when forced to turn right.
• Since for most green horses, turning to the left is easier than turning to the right, we start our daily sessions on the left rein.
• We usually start our lunging sessions on the left rein.
• Vaulting and most circus presentations are left bound.

In the first months of training, we have to live with the horse´s natural crookedness. Unless the horse is on the aids, we do not actually have the possibility of straightening without creating resistance and getting the horse tense. But towards the end of the first year, the young horse gradually understands the aids and will become more and more responsive.

The basic training aims for a horse that is pleasurable to ride, in harmony with his rider, and laterally and longitudinally well balanced. This includes the ability of the horse to move without effort on one track, the hind feet following the front feet on straight as well as curved lines.

A horse not moving absolutely straight, at whatever level, cannot be regarded as sufficiently trained.

The correctly straightened horse does not have an easy side and a difficult side. Each side should be equally pliable.

"Ride your horse forwards and straighten him", is the maxim of the German riding master Gustav Steinbrecht (1808–85). His book, *Gymnasium des Pferdes*, is the bible to the

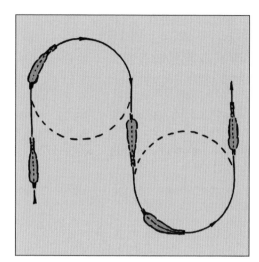

Fig. 31:The straightened horse can bend equally to both sides.

serious dressage trainer. His maxim sounds simple and logical, but to achieve it we must answer the question, "When is a horse straight?" To put it simply, *the horse is straight once there is laterally no difference in its flexibility to either side.* The horse knows how to bend to the right as well as to the left, and as a result the horse is able to adjust his body to straight as well as curved lines. The balanced horse does this by the indications of the aids.

The ability to move with front and hind feet on one track is of great importance for the later elements of the Training Tree. *Balance, Durchlässigkeit, Schwung, and collection cannot be achieved unless the horse is straightened.*

The relationship between straightness and **Schwung** is particularly noteworthy. A horse cannot properly exhibit **Schwung** unless he is straight first. Any car mechanic knows that in order for a car to pass an inspection, the wheels and axles must be straight. Without straightness, the car cannot run properly. The same principle applies to our horses. Asking for *Schwung* unless the horse is moving straight – "in the rails" – may compromise soudness.

Let us take a look at Figure 32. There is a train moving on the rails – just like the horse in Figure 31. The railway cars are pushed

Fig. 32: The straightened horse moves like a train that is being pushed from behind "on the rails". The power from the "engine" then is channelled and goes from the back to the front.

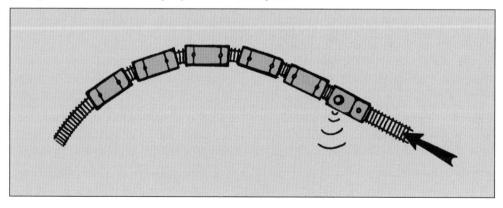

along the rails by the locomotive at the end of the train.

If we compare the railway cars with the horse´s spine and the locomotive with its hindquarters, we will realize the necessity of proper rails allowing the engine to channel all its power forward on both straight and curved lines. The rider, with his legs and reins, provides these rails so that the horse can use his engine (the hindquarters) without wasting energy.

If the rails are not in place, the train will derail. If the rails of the rider (legs and reins) are not in place, the horse will derail by falling out in front or behind. This is a serious fault, not to be confused with lateral work, which is not relevant at this stage of training.

How to achieve STRAIGHTNESS

As already mentioned, almost all horses move more or less crookedly by nature. Most of them are hollow to the right, which is sometimes called the soft side.

Actually, the hollow side is the tense side! The horse hollows the body to the right by contracting the muscles on that side. As a consequence, it leans on the left shoulder and won´t accept the right rein.

What straightening is all about is to *get the horse to release the muscles on the right side and to stretch for and accept the right rein.* Left-footed horses need the same kind of stretching but on the left side.

Any work on straightness needs a good seat and effective legs. The legs are asking and the hands are receiving. Dominating hands will spoil the flow of the motion and cause all kinds of evasions, like problems in the mouth, crossing the jaws, tilting at the poll, and possibly evading at the shoulders or the haunches.

A good seat allows the rider to keep his hands and legs steady, providing the rails the horse travels on. This way the rider keeps the horse balanced, controlling straightness on straight and curved lines. The rails prevent the horse from falling out with the shoulder or the haunches. A good rider can feel an attempt to evade and intervene before the evasion actually happens. Remember, effective aids are invisible!

This is similar to trying to balance a long bar vertically in the hand. At first, one needs to move the hand back and forth in all directions quite a lot. Later, after developing a feel for the balance, one can intervene almost invisibly before the tipping even starts.

In this state of training, there are many exercises for straightening a horse, like work on straight and curved lines, shallow loops, serpentines, and all kinds of circles. The effectiveness of such exercises depends, however, on their correct execution. *Riders who do not strive for precision in riding arena figures lack the self-discipline necessary for training a horse.*

Arena figures have been designed to help the horse and rider in the training. They give us the possibility for controlling our work.

The value of the straightening work lies in changing from one rein to the other. Horses that have a hard time bending to the left need more time on the left rein than the right. In order to avoid resistance, we must proceed carefully, never asking for more than the horse is ready to give.

The 20-metre circle is the most useful figure for introducing lateral bending to the horse. The horse develops the muscles and the skill to adjust to the moderately curved line. After a while, he will be able to remain within the rails on a 15-metre circle, and later on a 10-metre circle.

The Second Level horse can perform an eight-metre volte. The smallest circle a horse can perform without moving on two tracks is six-metres in diameter. This extreme flexion should not be expected before the horse has graduated to Third Level.

LEG-YIELDING – a basic exercise

Like the turn on the forehand, the *leg yield* is *not* a movement recommended for dressage horses above First Level. The reasons for this are that a) it is contradictory to the principle of adjusting the forehand to the haunches; and b) the horse is asked to move away from the leg instead of becoming engaged.

In *basic training*, however, mainly in Phase B, leg-yielding is highly recommended. It is a loosening and straightening exercise that demands quite a lot of sensitivity for co-ordi-nating the aids. It is also very educational for the young horse under a knowledgeable rider as well as for a beginner rider on a know-ledgeable horse. It develops the feel for co-ordinating the aids. At least one of the pair must know the job, otherwise both will become confused and end up in chaos.

Since the horse's legs are crossing there is no propulsive power created. This, however, can be very useful with a horse that is not in rhythm and rushing.

By making him cross his legs in a leg yield, we neutralize the propulsive power so that the horse will again listen to the aids for a calm and regular gait.

Any dressage movement has a certain *purpose*. The better the movement is executed, the better the purpose will be achieved. Consequently, leg-yielding will not lead to the desired result (looseness, straightness), unless correctly executed.

In the leg yield, the horse moves on two tracks forwards and sideways on an angle of 30–40 degrees from the forward direction. The horse yields from the left leg or from the right leg. According to the leg the horse is yielding from, we achieve the right-leg yield or the left-leg yield.

In the *right-leg yield* the horse moves to the left. In the *left-leg yield* the horse moves to the right. When the horse is yielding from the right leg, the right side is the inside. When the horse is yielding from the left leg, the left side is the inside.

In the leg yield the horse is relaxed and moves regularly and freely. He maintains con-

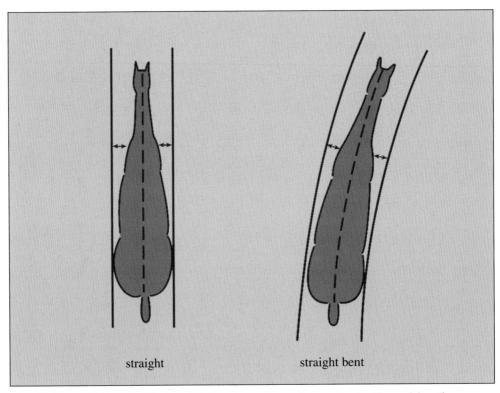

straight

straight bent

Fig. 33: The straight horse "within the rails". Note the equal spaces between the shoulders and the rails.

tact with the rider´s hand and doesn´t show any restriction in tempo and rhythm.

The body is straight from poll to tail, and the head is positioned to the inside. The horse is on the aids, thus ready to execute a turn on the forehand or a turn on the haunches, or to move straightforward and picking up a trot or canter.

In Figure 34, we see some examples for practising the leg yield:

a) Right-leg yield tracking left

b) Right-leg yield tracking right

c) Stairs: left leg yielding from centreline

d) Right-leg yield back and forth on the centreline, turn on the forehand without halting

e) Decreasing and increasing the arena by leg-yielding a symmetric figure (left-leg yield, straight ahead, right-leg yield)

Now, what does the correct leg-yielding horse look like? Take a look at Figure 35.

The horse yields from the *left* leg. The *left side* is the inside. The horse moves forwards to the *right* on an angle of 30–40 degrees. The horse´s body is straight, the head positioned to the left. The horse´s legs are crossing. The feet step on four lines.

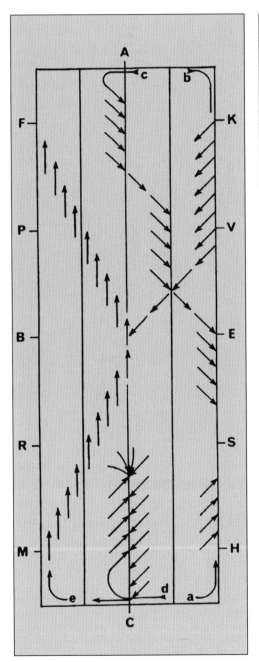

Fig. 34: Examples for leg-yielding. Please note that all these exercises should be ridden in a walk, the only exeption being "e", that can be ridden in a trot as well.

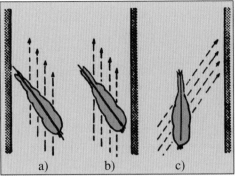

Fig. 35: Variations of leg-yielding
a) on the right rein
b) on the left rein
c) increasing the arena

Increasing the arena is the best way to introduce leg-yielding to the green horse.

On the centreline (Fig. 36), the leg-yielding horse may be asked to proceed

a) in a straightforward direction,

b) to transition to a turn on the forehand, or

c) to transition to a turn on the haunches.

In all these exercises the horse must be "in front of the rider", ready to move straightforward at any time. The turn on the haunches (c) is most educational since it corresponds to the principle of "adjusting to forehand to the haunches".

Note that all transitions from the leg yielding should end up with the horse being straight from poll to tail.

A transition to a circle, for example, contradicts the idea of the movement.

Also, do not use the leg yield with a transition from the shoulder-in! Here the horse is

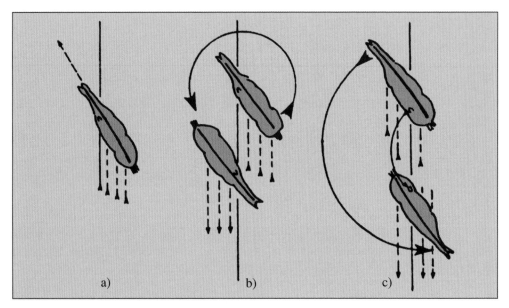

Fig. 36: Leg yielding left on the centreline, which can lead to a turn on the forehand or haunches:
(a) Leg-yielding in a 40-degree angle on the centreline
(b) Turn on the forehand (inside front foot on the centreline)
(c) Turn on the haunches (inside hind leg on the centreline)

laterally bent from poll to tail and therefore should transition into a circle or from the circle into the shoulder-in.

Unfortunately, there is still some confusion about the difference between leg-yielding and shoulder-in. Quite often in dressage tests one can see a "shoulder-in-like leg yield" or a "leg yield-like shoulder-in."

Remember the order of the elements in the Training Tree. By leg-yielding, we want to loosen the horse and to achieve straightness (Element 6). In shoulder-in, we want to improve Durchlässigkeit and achieve Schwung and collection (Elements 9 and 10). *Teaching shoulder-in unless the leg yield is confirmed is a big mistake.*

For this reason, I absolutely dislike movements in a dressage test that ask the leg-yielding horse to proceed to a circle. This is more confusing than educational for young riders and young horses. It leads the horse to evade by bending or falling out, thus facilitating the widespread misunderstanding of the difference between the leg yield and shoulder-in.

What are the aids for the leg yield? The *horse that is on the aids* is ready for leg-yielding. Properly on the bit, it will feel any deviation of the rider's seat and legs. We start at the walk. In order to make it easy, we turn down the centreline and ask the horse to yield from the left leg. The procedure (see Fig. 37), starts with the horse straight on the quarterline.

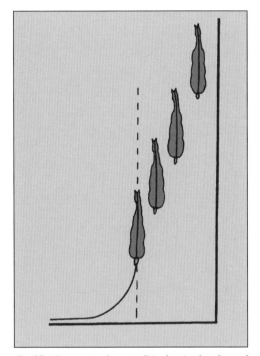

Fig 37: "Increasing the arena" is the simplest form of leg-yielding and can also be ridden at the trot.

• Then position the horse to the left by putting very little weight on the inside seat bone. The inside leg is just slightly behind the girth, the outside leg more so. The inside rein is a bit shorter so one can see the inner eyebrow (head position). The outside rein controls the outside shoulder to keep it from falling out.
• The inside leg asks the horse to yield while the outside leg supports forward momentum and controls the haunches from evading. The reins maintain position and control the outside shoulder for straightness.

The transition from leg-yielding to the halt (at the wall) is also quite educational, since the rider develops the feel of getting the inside hind foot in place.

The most frequent faults for horse and rider include the following:

Rider: Getting tense, twisting in the body, collapsing in the hip, inside seat bone not in place, inside leg too far back, lack of effectiveness, poor timing, outside leg out of place, lack of forward momentum, pulling on the inner rein, and no contact with the outside rein.

Horse: Fighting the bit, crossing the jaws, tilting at the poll or neck, moving irregularly, altering tempo, and evading by falling out over the outside shoulder by dragging and not crossing the hind feet, and swinging out the haunches.

To sum it up, the leg yield is indispensable for loosening and straightening the horse in *basic training*. The value of the movement, however, lies in its correct execution, and this is more difficult than it may seem.

Therefore keep this warning in mind: do not ask a rider to leg yield unless the seat is confirmed and the horse is on the aids. In order to work on straightness, the horse must first be on the aids (Element 5 before Element 6).

The work on straightness includes **riding in position**. This is because the horse that is not straightened, travelling along the wall of the arena, tends to fall in or out with the shoulder (Fig. 38). Imagine the first car of the train derailing. In this way the power of the engine is blocked and cannot go through. The forward momentum is restricted. In order to get

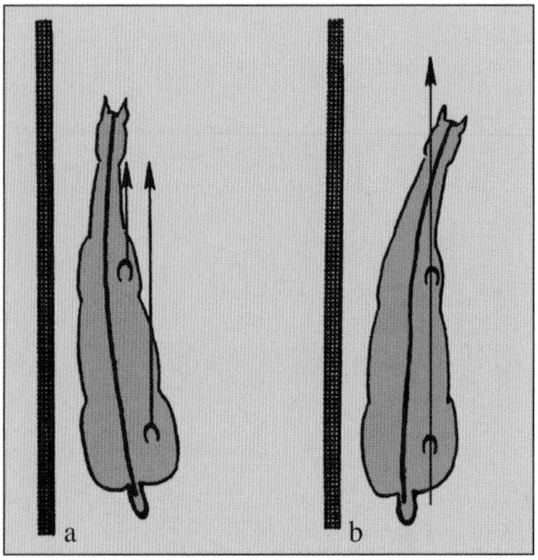

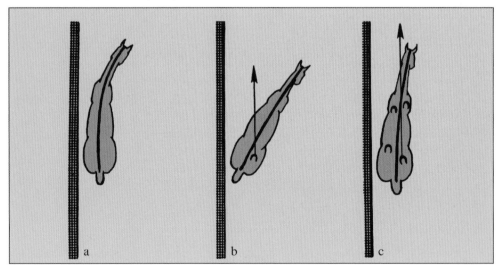

Fig. 38: Wrong! Because of natural crookedness, the horse leans against the wall with its shoulder! The push from the inside hind is lost. Corrections: By riding in position the horse gets straightened by adjusting the forehand to the hindquarters. Inside fore and inside hind stay on the track and the push is not interrupted.

the horse within the rails again, we need to *adjust the forehand to the quarters*, which is a basic principle in dressage! We place the inside shoulder of the horse in front of the inside hind foot so that both the inside hind foot and the inside front foot are moving on *one line*. By adjusting the forehand to the haunches (and not the haunches to the forehand), we respect the priority of the haunches, which is where all propulsive power originates.

When riding in position the rider should feel an increased responsivness from the inside leg. At the poll the horse's head is slightly flexed to the inside, so the rider can just see the inside eyebrow and the inside nostril (as in leg-yielding). In canter work, the horse is always positioned to the inside.

Fig. 39: The shoulder fore, for straightness, along the wall.
a) Wrong! The neck is pulled to the inside, the horse withdraws from the aids and the exercise is of no value!
b) Wrong! Leg-yield-like shoulder fore, no thrust from behind.
c) Correct! Body slightly bent to the inside, push under control. The tailbone stays parallel to the wall.
The inside hind steps between the forelegs.

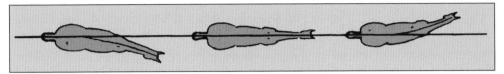

Fig. 40: Shoulder fore on the centreline. By adjusting the forehand to the hindquarters, the rider first brings the right, then the left shoulder fore; the hindlegs stay on line.

The next step in straightening the horse is the **shoulder fore**. This exercise is more difficult, but its gymnastic effect is bigger than riding in position. We place the inside shoulder a bit more to the inside so that the inside front foot steps on a separate line. The exercise is useless and even damaging if the rider just pulls the neck to the inside (a common fault). The horse´s body needs to be very slightly bent to the inside, the neck being just a part of the bend, so that the inside hind foot steps in the direction between the front feet (Fig. 39).

The shoulder fore also prepares the horse for the shoulder-in, which we may apply towards the end of the second year of basic training when working on **Schwung** and collection (Elements 9 and 10).

For riding in position or shoulder fore you need help from the ground. Standing at the end of the line you are working on, the ground person can evaluate the correctness of the movement. If you are fortunate enough to have a mirror in your arena, you should use it for refining the movement.

Riding in counter-position is a helpful exercise for straightening the horse. It can be practised on straight lines as well as on a 20-metre circle. The movement is most effective

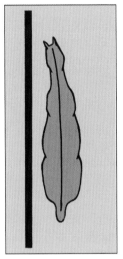 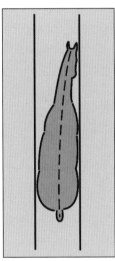

Fig. 41: Counter-position for stretching the right side.

Fig. 42: Riding in (right) position: inside hip, inside shoulder, inside eyelash/nostril on the "right-side rail".

for stretching the hollow side and improving the rein contact on this side.

Assume that your horse tends to travel crookedly. He is not accepting the inside (right) rein as he leans with the outside (left) shoulder on the left rein. His inside (right) hind is not within the rails and evades to the inside (Fig. 41).

For correction we ride in counter-position while imagining the wall to be on our right side (Fig. 42).

BALANCE

THE SEVENTH ELEMENT OF THE TRAINING TREE

"There is no secret so close as that between a rider and his horse." (Robert Smith Surtees)

Horse and rider are well balanced once there is equal weight and power on both sides and a common centre of gravity at all times. Like any object in balance, the horse becomes light in the hand and easy to handle. Consequently, the rider can maintain balance in all movements by feel and skill rather than by physical force.

There is lateral and longitudinal balance that affects the horse in motion. Since lateral balance is prerequisite for longitudinal balance, let us discuss it first.

Lateral balance can be expected once *straightness* (Element 6) is achieved. The straightened horse that bends easily to both sides by minimal aids and travels within the rails at all times (right rail: right leg and rein; left rail: left leg and rein), is laterally balanced. The rider is able to check this balance by taking the reins in one hand while riding on straight and curved lines. If the rider can maintain contact and stay on one track, the horse is laterally balanced.

Let us discuss for a moment taking the reins in one hand. Beginning with a horse that is not completely straightened, the rider may hold the reins (in both hands) a bit wider. This

way he gives the horse some support and helps him find his balance. However, once the horse is able to stay in balance, he does not need that support from the rider. The rider should always strive to carry the hands close together, enclosing the neck. At its best, the horse should not feel any difference when the reins are held in one or both hands.

In dressage tests, we often see riders compensating for a lack of straightness by balancing with widely set hands – even at the higher levels! This reminds me of a tightrope walker who needs a long pole to stay in balance.

Fig. 43: The well-balanced bicycle (or horse) does not need to be supported by the hands. When the balance is lost on the bicycle (or horse) the upper body and arms have to help regain the balance.

Without this support, he would fall, just as the crooked horse would fall out of balance without the support of the rider´s hands. Dressage judges are well advised to keep an eye on this basic requirement.

Skiing also requires similar balancing skills to those in riding. But when a skier has a severe lack of balance, he ends up with his head in the snow. It's useless to blame the skis.

Horses, however, get out of balance due to poor riding and yet carry on faithfully. They just try to compensate for the lack of balance by leaning on one rein or by moving on two tracks. They certainly don´t deserve to be blamed for this "bad habit".

Regrettably, our dressage tests do not ask for movements done on one hand anymore. Without any doubt, this was a step in the wrong direction. We may end up allowing draw reins in the tests because people will become unable to get horses on the bit.

Carrying the hands close together is even more necessary when using the double bridle. (Of course the double bridle cannot be used before the successful completion of basic training.) The non-broken curb bit does not allow any unevenness in using the reins. That´s why the horse must be confirmed in balance and self-carriage before using the double bridle. This sophisticated instrument is a tool only for the hand of a sensitive rider and is used for refining the rein aids when asking for collection.

A useful way to think about balance is in the example of a bicycle (Fig. 43). Everyone knows how to ride a bicycle. When riding

without hands, we need a bike that is mechanically well adjusted. If not, we must compensate for the lack of balance by bending the body to the side opposite from which the bike is deviating. Since this is uncomfortable, we compensate for lack of balance by holding one handlebar against the deviation. When driving a badly adjusted car, we permanently steer against the tendency to deviate.

When a rider tries to compensate for such deviations in an unbalanced horse that leans to the left, the rider often hangs on the left rein (ending up with a sore arm), or collapses in the left hip.

The latter is a rather common fault.

Bikes and cars that aren´t properly balanced can be fixed in the next repair shop. However, horses that have problems with balance cannot just be repaired. They need to be straightened by daily work from the saddle, riding all those basic movements again and again. These exercises build up the flexibility necessary for proper lateral balance. There are no shortcuts or tricks to building balance.

Longitudinal balance enables the horse to become lighter in the forehand, which can be considered once the horse is laterally balanced. Until this point, the horse moves more or less *on the forehand*. This is acceptable since to develop a good topline and a swinging back, we give priority to all those movements that help get the horse´s muscles relaxed and stretched. Early in the horse´s training we allow the horse to stretch the neck well forwards and downwards and do not care so much about the additional weight the front

Fig. 44: A well-balanced horse trustingly jumps with minimum effort.
The author on "Alpenmärchen", eventing in Luhmühlen, Germany.

feet have to carry. In Phase B of training, the hind feet *push* and develop propulsive power rather than *carry*.

Phase C of the Training Tree asks for the development of carriage and lightness. In this phase, once the horse is laterally balanced, we need to get the hindquarters en-gaged. The horse must learn to step under the centre of gravity more, thus taking more weight off the body and relieving the forehand.

In this way the laterally and longitudinally balanced horse returns to his natural gaits, which until this point had been restricted by the rider´s weight. Now the horse is ready for work on *Durchlässigkeit* and *Schwung* (Elements 8 and 9) and may be asked for the first steps in collection (Element 10).

Full harmony requires that the horse and rider are in balance and share *a centre of gravity* in all movements. I always have a hard time tolerating dressage riders who position their horses to one side while they themselves are looking to the other side. This violates the harmony. Let me recommend this rule: The rider's nose and the horse´s nose are coordinated and should always face in the same direction.

As mentioned before, the double bridle should *not* be used unless the horse is laterally and longitudinally balanced, *durchlässig*, and knows how to respond to half-halts. Using the curb bit before this stage leads to disharmony and results in tension and resistance. The only reason for using the double bridle is to refine the aids on the way to collection in a well-balanced horse. This can-

not be expected before the end of the second year of a solid basic training.

The double bridle is *not*, as is often seen, for getting the horse on the bit!

Unfortunately, many riders who are unable to get their horses properly on the bit in a plain snaffle, use the double bridle, and thus put the horse in a straightjacket. Some even *show* their horses this way. This is a gross violation of the principles of classical dressage and of the Training Tree.

The Prix St. James test is designed to reduce the number of riders showing at FEI levels without sufficient grounding in the basics. This combined dressage test is meant to be the first of a two-part test (the second is the Prix St. Georg test), and requires that the absolutely balanced horse be presented in the plain snaffle.

The Prix St. James encourages the competitors to take more time with the *basics*. Qualified judges and trainers realize the value of a solid foundation, which is beneficial for the horses and indispensable for successful international competition.

The balanced horse is a pleasure to ride. Beginner riders should be given the opportunity to ride such horses so that they will get an idea of the feeling.

Once balance is achieved, however, it doesn´t last forever. Again and again, balance must be re-established through systematic work on straightness, which, as we know, is an essential part of the daily warm-up.

When working on *balance*, you must aim for perfection so that your aids become invisible. The laterally and longitudinally well-balanced horse can move as if it were dancing on a tightrope with minimal support. Once in a while, reassure yourself of the proper balance by taking the reins in one hand when executing movements or by **überstreichen**. This German term has been explained in the USDF Glossary of Judging Terms like this: "Loosening of the reins by moving the hands forward along the horse´s neck, to demonstrate that the horse is in self carriage – neither increasing nor decreasing the pace, nor changing the balance or outline". Serious disobedience (stopping, turning, rearing)

often starts with the horse refusing to stay within the rails and not staying in front of the legs.

The properly balanced horse stays *in the rails* at all times, and is thus confident and obedient. There is a permanent common centre of gravity of horse and rider that enables the pair to execute movements with lightness and ease, on the flat as well as when jumping. When you are in complete balance and harmony with your horse, you have the opportunity to understand and verify Colonel Alois Podhajsky's insight: "The rider thinks – the horse executes."

DURCHLÄSSIGKEIT
THE EIGHTS ELEMENT OF
THE TRAINING TREE

"Aim for positive co-operation of your horse rather than submission."

Let us again look at the Training Tree. By now we have discussed seven elements, and we know – at least in theory – how to proceed until the horse and rider are well balanced. As we know, it will take more than one year to achieve this, and it will require patience and discipline. Shortcuts provoke problems. They endanger the health of the young horse, damaging his confidence and willingness, thus affecting his personality. In most cases, it ends up in disappointment.

Good trainers know how to tune the training to correspond with the progressing maturity of the horse. His health and willingness are a treasure that can´t be made the subject of a deal for getting a blue ribbon.

Following the sequence in the Training Tree, the next element to be considered is *Durchlässigkeit*. This eighth element cannot be expected unless both horse and rider are in balance (Element 7). Balance, as we know, depends on straightness (Element 6), which again cannot be confirmed unless all preceding elements have been sufficiently confirmed.

Let me emphasize again that *Durchlässigkeit* (often translated as suppleness), is not looseness. It is much more! "Suppleness is the physical ability of the horse to shift the point of equilibrium smoothly forwards and back as well as laterally without stiffness or resistance. Suppleness is manifested by the horse´s fluid response to the rider´s restraining and positioning aids of the rein and to the driving aids of legs and seat. Suppleness is best judged in transition" (AHSA *Rule Book*).

Another definition reads, *Durchlässigkeit* is "pliability, showing ability to smoothly adjust the carriage (longitudinally) and the position or bend (laterally) without impairment of the flow of movement or the balance" (USDF *Glossary of Judging Terms*).

Those two definitions are not quite satisfactory, which is why in this book, I prefer to use the German term, *Durchlässigkeit*.

In addition to the above explanations, **Durchlässigkeit** means that there is a permanent connection between the hind feet and hands that allows the energy to flow back and forth throughout the horse like water in the garden hose. This way the thrust from the hindquarters goes through the body to be received by the hands, and the signals from the hands go through to reach and influence the hindquarters without resistance.

This circulation of energy, *created by the rider's driving seat and legs*, only works once there is no barrier that impedes the flow.

Barriers arise from stiffness, which comes from a lack of systematic work on relaxation, (Element 1). Relaxation must be achieved in each training session before starting serious work with the horse.

Barriers can occur along the back at the mouth, jaw, or poll, as well as any muscle or joint throughout the horse's body. Removing these barriers by force is not in harmony with the principles of good horsemanship, since it creates fear, pain and resistance. This is discussed further in the chapter on Element 1, relaxation.

No horse should be considered supple or **durchlässig** unless there is a connection between the hindquarters and the hand. The horse must be on the aids (Element 5), responding instantly to legs and seat while maintaining a steady contact with the hands, thus allowing the energy to circulate.

The key to this lies in the rider's ability to make the circulation of energy happen. It is the *rider* who must first of all be connected and supple before he or she can develop suppleness in the horse. The *rider* is the one to ride the horse into balance and to create the energy desired. Once the rider receives this energy in the hands, the rider can transmit it back to the haunches, thus closing the circle.

As you can see, this procedure is already the essential point of the **half-halt**, which is the key method for responsiveness in the dressage horse.

Through half-halts, we control regularity pace and balance. We recall the horse to attention and we re-establish the circle of energy, thus improving *engagement and suppleness*.

Prior to any transition to another bend, gait or movement, we ensure by a half-halt that the horse is supple enough to perform a smooth transition. If the half-halt doesn't come through as desired, we try it again and again until we feel an instant reaction. Without a clear response to the half-halt, we should not ride *any* transition because it would not work out properly. The horse must be *ready* for the next movement before we ask for the execution.

It is like an electric circuit that must be completed before we can expect power to go through it.

Without power and connection, the light bulb cannot go on.

For a proper downward transition, we also need the circuit to make sure that the hindquarters stay engaged while the hands are giving signals that are well coordinated with the motion. Riders who just "pull the plug" without giving the horse sufficient preparation cannot complain about the horse falling apart.

We ask for the closed halt in the same way. The horse at the closed halt has a posture "in which the horse is secure in balance and in attitude, and has the hind legs sufficiently under the body so that the weight of the horse and rider is distributed evenly overall for legs" (USDF *Glossary of Judging Terms*).

The better the *Durchlässigkeit* (or suppleness), the fewer half-halts we need for the closed halt. "Suppleness is best judged in transitions."

The aids for a good half-halt are hardly visible. The supple and well-balanced horse responds to the *engaged seat* (see On the Seat in the chapter "On the Aids") and the asking leg. He gets light in the forehand and is receptive at the mouth.

Beginner riders have a hard time learning to ride an effective half-halt. It is almost impossible to teach this key aid on a poorly trained horse. The rider must have the chance to ride an old schoolmaster who knows his job. Horses are the best teachers.

Once your horse responds to the half-halt instantly and without resistance, you can increase the engagement of the hindquarters. By increasing the activity in the hindquarters, you move on to creating *Schwung* (often translated as impulsion). (Element 9)

SCHWUNG
THE NINTH ELEMENT OF THE TRAINING TREE

"The thrust of the haunches must be channelled by keeping the horse within the rails."

Schwung is a German term that is often translated as impulsion. **Schwung** is "the powerful thrust emanating from the hindquarters propelling the horse forwards and travelling through an elastic, swinging back and a relaxed neck. It demonstrates the horse´s elasticity and desire to carry himself and spring off the ground" (USDF *Glossary of Judging Terms*).

Prerequisite for the work on *Schwung* is sufficiently developed *Durchlässigkeit* (Element 8) and a rider who knows how to apply the half-halt.

Schwung only shows in gaits that have a phase of suspension, in which the horse has no feet on the ground. The more impulsion the rider is able to mobilize, the longer the phase of suspension. Trot and canter will become lighter and more brilliant. **Schwung** (impulsion) cannot be created at walk, since the horse switches between two-leg support and three-leg support. In other words there is no suspension at the walk.

The proper response to half-halts is the key for creating **Schwung**. With half-halts we generate more energy from the hindquarters. Once we feel the response desired by more carriage, lightness and suspension, we allow the horse to express this energy through the extension.

Occasionally I am asked, "My horse does all the movements fine, he just does not do trot extensions. Can you help me?" After watching the rider´s work for a short time, I may observe that the horse is moving crookedly and unevenly. Or I may notice a tense back, short gaits, or a lack of **Durchlässigkeit** and **Schwung**. In all these cases, my answer is similar to this: "Sorry, I can´t help you right now. Your horse lacks all the prerequisites for the extensions. Return to the basics, acquire a solid foundation before you even think of extensions. The Training Tree will help. See you next spring."

Unfortunately, we still see horses showing upper-level movements without a sufficient foundation. These horses have been drilled in a straightjacket. They have learned all the tricks but in doing so, they have lost their natural freedom, lightness and beauty. This kind of "dressage" is disgusting and should not be tolerated in the show ring.

People sometimes think that **Schwung** results just from engaging the hindquarters.

This is not incorrect, but it is not the whole story either. The essential point of **Schwung** is the *swinging back* that makes it a pleasure for the rider. On a swinging back, the rider can follow the waves of the back to produce **Schwung** and suspension. It is the *Rückengänger* (the backmover) that allows **Schwung** to go through and makes extreme lengthening a pleasure for both rider and horse, as well as for spectators.

The *Schenkelgänger* (leg mover) may move the legs spectacularly, but without the participation of the back. That is why his rider cannot sit the movement. Pinching the legs and stiffening the body, the rider tries to survive the "breathtaking lengthenings". Good judges will not be impressed with this kind of "big mover".

For developing *Schwung*, the horse must be within the rails and the rider must have a good feel for the tempo and regularity of the gaits. The purity of these two elements should never be compromised or tampered with.

After **Schwung** has been confirmed, the rider may think of improving the cadence of the motion, that is, "the marked accenting of the rhythm with elasticity".

Like *Durchlässigkeit*, *Schwung* is an element of Phase C of the Training Tree, which covers Second Level movements. The transition from First to Second Level is gradual. The more you achieve **Durchlässigkeit** and **Schwung**, the more the horse develops towards Second Level.

When the rider asks for *Schwung*, it is helpful to keep the following in mind. "Impulsion has to be maintained by consecutive, more or less accentuated, and yet soft pressure of the rider´s lower legs at the girth in rhythm with his movement. Unquiet hands and exaggerated body movements disturb the horse´s equilibrium and are detrimental to calm and to fluency of the movement" (*A Dressage Judge´s Handbook*, K. A. von Ziegner).

Highly gifted horses excluded, we should not expect true *Durchlässigkeit* and *Schwung* before the last half-year of basic training. Once these elements are confirmed, we may gradually start to include work on collection in our daily sessions.

COLLECTION

THE TENTH ELEMENT OF
THE TRAINING TREE

"Where violence begins – art ends." (Colonel Bengt Ljungquist)

Towards the end of the first year of *basic training,* our prospect is four and a half years old and *on the aids*. He trusts his rider and travels with confidence in the walk, trot and canter in his natural frame. He is familiar with cavalletti work and loves to jump small fences on the flat as well as in the country. Since we included work on *straightness* (Element 6) in the daily sessions, our horse has become more and more balanced (Element 7), and thus ready to be shown in First Level dressage competitions.

In the second year our horse is turning five. He is no baby anymore. He is sound, well muscled and eager to work. He is on the way to Second Level.

In the second year we confirm all the elements acquired in the first year and focus on *Durchlässigkeit* and *Schwung* (Elements 8 and 9), elements that make the horse ready for the first attempts at collection (Element 10). The Second Level horse is ready to adapt to a Second Level frame at any time. The horse is gathered together and therefore the outline appears shorter. The horse takes more weight on the hindquarters, thus becoming more elevated in the forehand. Longitudinal-

ly balanced, he shows more carriage, his movements become more cadenced, and his engagement becomes more marked (Fig. 45).

To get to this point, we must proceed carefully. It usually takes one year to develop the necessary muscles the horse needs to maintain engagement and to carry himself. The hind feet, which in the first year had mainly *propelled the horse forwards* (Phase B of the Training Tree), must now be asked to step more under the *centre of gravity* (Phase C).

I like the way Violet Hopkins, the First Lady of American dressage, puts it:

"When the horse has accepted the rider´s hand and stretches to the bit, the rider must be aware that the next step is to make the engagement greater, rounding the back more and not allowing the horse to remain on the forehand. With more engagement of the hindquarters, roundness of the back and flexion at the poll should appear.

"As the horse gains strength and muscle control, the centre of balance changes more to the hindquarters. The forehand becomes more elevated, and the weight is more evenly distributed on all four feet. From this point, the horse is ready for collection. From this

Fig. 45: Frames in canter
Left: natural canter (Phase A)
Right: collected canter (after basic training has been concluded).

stage on, the rider´s understanding and ability to ride determines the progress to the higher levels."

At the **halt**, the collected horse becomes more closed so that, at its best, there is a vertical line from the point of the hip to the toe of the hind foot (Fig. 47).

Collection is the result of special training by an experienced rider, who knows that any engagement from behind cannot work unless the horse is connected from behind onto the bit by a stretched topline and a swinging back.

Horses differ in their ability to collect according to their physical and mental confirmation. There are horses that are highly talented and there are horses that are not talented at all. One can teach any horse more or less dressage, but not every horse is a dressage horse.

In purchasing a dressage prospect, we pay special attention to the ability to collect, rather than the "breathtaking trot". Many horses, when turned out free with tails up, show that kind of trot, which comes from excitement and tension. We should not be impressed by this. It is *the ability to collect* we want to see when the horse is playing around.

We want to see the way he balances and how he uses his hind feet in turns and stops, because in the higher levels, it is *collection* that counts, expressing accuracy, lightness and elegance.

Studies have been made about the best physical conformation and about the ideal angles in the forehand and hindquarters of a dressage horse. I think one should not overestimate those measurements. It is not a statue for the park we want to buy. We are

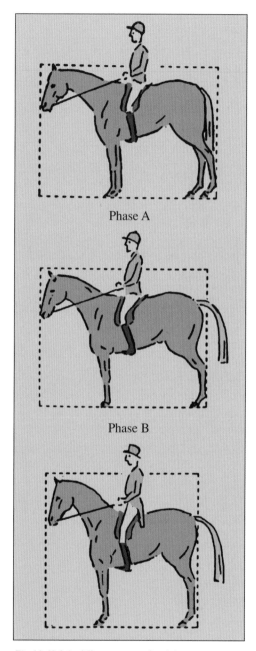

Phase A

Phase B

Fig 46: Halt in different stages of training:
  in Phase A ("open")
  in Phase B ("on the aids")
  in Phase C ("closed")

looking for a horse that knows how to move. The highly talented dressage prospect that is balanced from nature and dances under the rider right away is an exception and must be regarded as a gift from nature. We need to handle that gift with special care. It takes much self-discipline and understanding not to accept the collection offered before the horse is mentally and physically ready for the tenth element of the Training Tree.

Unfortunately, we still see riders who, for whatever reason, take advantage of the young-ster´s willingness to collect. Violating the principles of basic training, they show even in the upper levels, risking the horse´s health and reputation. This way, quite a number of gifted prospects end up with problems before even maturing.

Perfect collection is *not* the object of *basic training*. We just introduce the new element by asking for more engagement, and we are satisfied with more carriage resulting from the increased activity of the hind feet. We want to feel the energy swinging throughout the horse, and we want to be able to regulate rhythm and balance by receiving this energy in the hands. Any force applied is wrong, since it would provoke tension and resistance.

It requires quite a lot of riding experience to teach collection without getting the horse tense or defensive. As we know, the horse in nature does not move in a collected way, except for short periods when excited. The horse in nature moves with a stretched neck and the hind feet pushing rather than carry-ing the body.

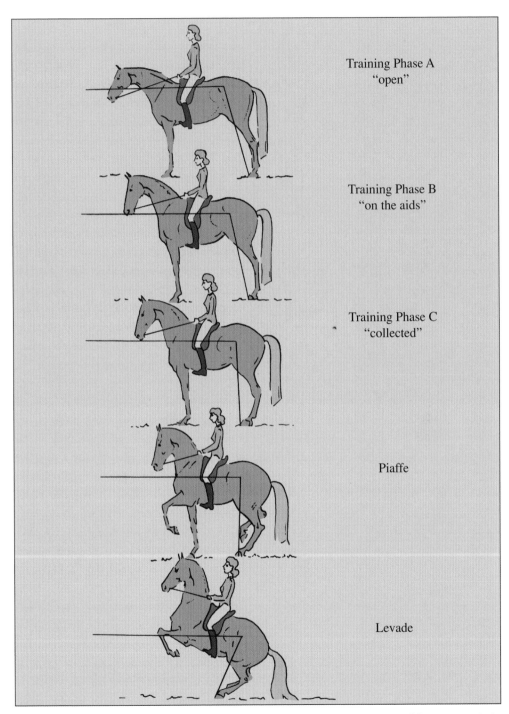

Training Phase A
"open"

Training Phase B
"on the aids"

Training Phase C
"collected"

Piaffe

Levade

Fig. 47: The principle of collection according to W. Müseler. Note that raising and elevation of the movements is the result of the ability to bend the hocks and lower the croup. "The bow in front of the rider (the neck) results from the bow behind the rider (the haunches)."

Knowing this, we must realize that collected gaits are actually "artificial gaits", which need to be taught. There are quite different muscles required for collection, and they must be gradually developed.

Asking a horse for more engagement from behind is a normal process on the way to Second Level. Provided that all the elements of the Training Tree are sufficiently achieved, unexpected difficulties should not arise.

Now let us take a look at Figure 47.

This graphic representation comes from Wilhem Müseler's book, *Riding Logic*, which was first published in 1933. It has been translated from German into ten different languages. The graphics from this famous book have been cited and reproduced in equestrian literature many times, because there is no better way to make these issues understandable.

A horse *on the aids* (Element 5) that is *straightened* (Element 6), *balanced* (Element 7), *durchlässig* (Element 8), and develops *Schwung* (Element 9) is ready for *collection*. As mentioned before, this order is not only the guideline for the second year of *basic training*. It also must be the guideline for the daily sessions.

Each session begins with work on *relaxation* (Element 1), and each session must end with a relaxed and happy horse.

The key for *collection* lies in the skill to ride the *half-halt* properly and to use this unique tool in co-ordination with the horse's motion. Needless to say, a half-halt can only come through in a horse that is straightened and within the rails.

By engaging the seat (or tipping the barrel) and asking with the legs, we mobilize the hind feet, using the hands to transform this increased activity into *collection*. The hind feet, which were used to *propel the horse forwards*, are now asked to step more under the centre of gravity and to carry more weight. This way, the horse becomes lighter in the forehand and more receptive to the aids.

But remember that elevation must always be a result of lowering the haunches. Otherwise it would look like Figure 48.

Since lowering the haunches is not possible unless the horse is balanced, supple and moving with Schwung, we reassure ourselves of the quality of these elements repeatedly with half-halts before we ask the horse to collect.

Transitions of all kinds, decreasing and increasing circles, the eight-metre volte, shoulder-in, and counter canter are useful exercises to make the horse **durchlässig** and thus capable to collect. Bending haunches and half steps are not subjects of basic training.

Moving in collected gaits is hard work for the horse. That's why we maintain the increased engagement at first for just short periods so that the horse can relax and the strained muscles can recover. Unevenness and tension indicate insufficient physical development for collection.

Chewing the bit out of the hand is an indispensable exercise for checking for a relaxed back after work on *collection*. The well-trained horse can demonstrate this exercise at walk, trot and canter, no matter what the level. This is why the Prix St. James test

Fig 48: Misunderstood "elevation". The whole body of the horse is tense, the hocks are not bent, there is no sign of collection.

asks explicitly for this basic exercise. Dr. Reiner Klimke´s world champion *Ahlerich* was exemplary in this aspect.

The double bridle is *not* a tool to enforce *collection*. A rider who is not able to collect his or her horse on the plain snaffle must learn how to do it. The double bridle serves just for the refinement of the aids once the horse has learned to carry himself. Judges must have an eye for that and the courage to mark it down! The Prix St. James will facilitate the evaluation.

Riders who obviously torture the horse into collection must be told to be fair.

Introducing the horse to collection is the last part of basic training. At its end the horse has accomplished an all-around training process. He is sound in mind and body, he expresses confidence in the rider, and he is willing to perform that which is asked of him. He is ready for Second Level dressage competition and is familiar with jumping all kinds of small fences on the flat as well as out in the country.

Now the door for **special training** at the higher levels is open. No matter what discipline we choose – dressage, jumping, eventing – we will pursue a well-planned programme, always tuned to the present capability of our horse, keeping him sound and willing to work. This is the safest way of achieving further success.

REFLECTIONS ON SCHOOL FIGURES

"Do not force accuracy. Strive for it."

Good instructors spend a lot of energy reminding their students to ride proper school figures. This is because a permanent effort to ride these figures precisely is of great value in both schooling the rider as well as in training the horse.

They require the rider to apply the aids properly, and they reveal to the instructor the progress of his student. The rider learns to concentrate on feel and accuracy. The horse develops the muscles and skills necessary for doing his job under the rider with the minimum of effort.

School figures have been designed and handed down to us by the old masters. We can find the patterns in The *Principles of Riding* (the official handbook for German instructors), and in *Riding Logic* by Wilhelm Müseler. Both books are recommended by the USDF.

School figures are no end in themselves. They are the best means of training a horse and absolutely indispensable for the education of the rider. The horse is made attentive and alert to the aids of the rider, who should instantly be aware of any deviation from the desired track.

Only by striving for correct school figures will the horse and rider profit from each other. Beginner riders should practise at first in the indoor school, since there are no distractions for the horse. Once they have enough control for riding decent figures, they must confirm this skill under different conditions.

Serious riders know the value of the school figures. Aiming for perfect execution, they concentrate on improving their position and on fine-tuning the aids. Self-discipline, a calm seat and invisible aids are good prerequisites for the desired co-operation of the horse.

The letters on the wall of the indoor school are well known, but they are absolutely useless when not respected.

They often represent the beginning or end of a figure, movement or gait. It takes a lot of practice to ride to the letter!

In Germany, some of the letters (H, K, F, and M) and the markers for the circle are called *Paradepunkte* (half-halt points). At these points we check for *balance, Durchlässigkeit* and *Schwung* with half-halts. I like to call these points check points.

Riders who want to compete in dressage must be accustomed to riding to the letters.

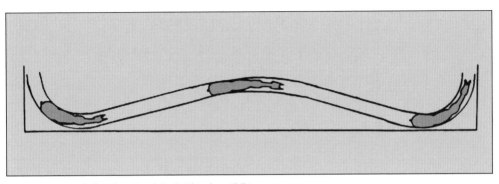

Fig. 49: Correct shallow loop (straight "within the rails").

A "Halt at C" means the rider´s body is at the letter and the horse is halted, and "At A – Working canter" means the first canter stride must start at A, not one or two metres later. This simple homework proves its worth in the test. Such accuracy should be second nature, because during the test the rider must concentrate on many things other than riding correct corners. Riding correct figures should be automatic.

Diagonals and other connecting lines must be straight, circles must be evenly round, and serpentines must be symmetrical. That sounds so simple, but it is not! Most people have a hard time even drawing these patterns by hand.

Green riders need visual assistance to learn how to perform these figures. Cones, poles laid on the ground, and lines raked in the sand are excellent tools for developing the necessary feel for co-operation between rider and horse.

Exercising school figures on recently raked ground is exciting and educational, since it gives the rider the unique opportunity to control his own performance.

Fig. 50: Left: crocked on a straight line. Right: stiff like a ship on the turn.

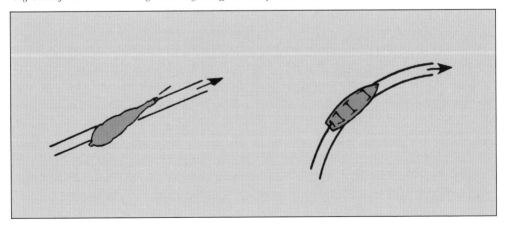

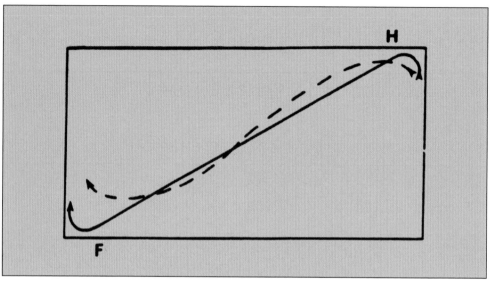

Fig. 51: Changing direction on the diagonal.
Correct: Straight from point H to point F. Wrong: To weave around the direct line.

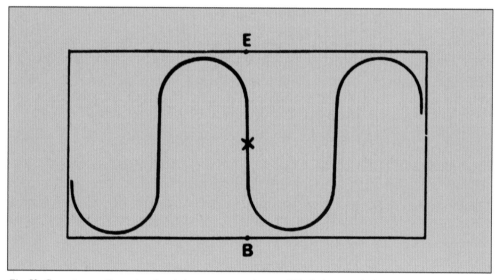

Fig. 52: Correct serpentines using the whole arena are much more difficult than one thinks.

Except for the leg yield, school figures in basic training are ridden on one track. When the horse is on one track, he stays within the rails on straight as well as curved lines. As we know, this requires a great deal of lateral pliability for the horse (*see Straightness*, Element 6).

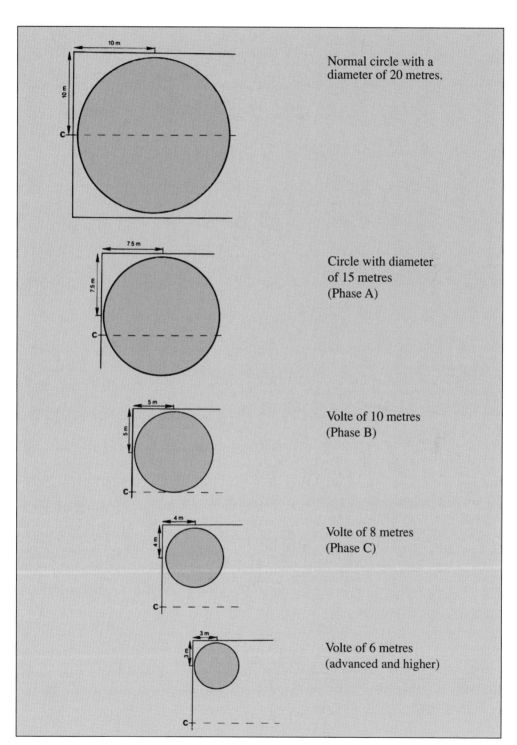

Normal circle with a diameter of 20 metres.

Circle with diameter of 15 metres (Phase A)

Volte of 10 metres (Phase B)

Volte of 8 metres (Phase C)

Volte of 6 metres (advanced and higher)

Fig. 53: Circles, voltes and corners, adapted to the phase of training by the diameter.

Crooked or stiff horses cannot adjust to the track, and that is why they derail and fall outside of the rails.

Unfortunately, there are still horses in dressage shows that move in this way, even at the upper levels. Judges may take care of that.

School figures make flat work more educational and more interesting. Trainers who do not care about this lack seriousness. They neither have a system in their teaching nor any control over the progress of their students.

Corners are school figures. Properly executed, the corner is a quarter section of a six-metre volte, which is the smallest circle a horse can perform without moving on two tracks.

A correct corner needs the utmost of lateral bend. It is clear that deeper corners are ridden in higher education (Fig. 53). "A rider who knows how to ride a corner knows almost all about riding." This quotation has a lot of truth to it. In a corner the rider must be able to ride half-halts properly, know how to bend the horse, and know how to maintain *Durchlässigkeit*, rhythm, and *Schwung*. Is this not almost all there is to know about dressage?

REFLECTIONS ON SCHOOL MOVEMENTS

"The horse and rider must be good craftsmen before becoming artists."

Following the guideline of the Training Tree, it takes about two years to get the green horse acquainted and comfortable with the rider and up to the achievement of the first collection.

We must respect the rules of the Training Tree and proceed carefully and systematically, thus building up a solid foundation for further special training. As we pro-gress in the daily dressage work, we use school figures and school movements suitable for developing the desired elements of the Training Tree Remember that relaxation, regularity, freedom and contact are always the priority. If any of these elements suffer, the trainer must return to more basic work to prepare the horse again.

In most books on riding you can find something about the various movements used in dressage. From pictures, you can see how the movements look and you can get information about how to apply the aids. For our purposes here I will assume that you know what they are and how to do them. What I will discuss is:

• *What* are the appropriate movements in the different phases of training?

• *Why* are they helpful?

• *When* is it productive to use them, and when not?

Before going into details, I must stress our basic principle again that green riders should learn from schooled horses, and green horses learn best from experienced riders. The one who teaches must know the job. If both horse and rider are inexperienced it cannot work. In most cases it leads to frustration.

For better comprehension, we need to review the Training Tree. There are three different phases in *basic training*.

Phase A (on the way to Training Level): the horse becomes accustomed to the rider´s weight.

Phase B (on the way to First Level): the horse develops propulsive power (*Schubkraft*).

Phase C (on the way to Second Level): the horse develops carriage (*Tragkraft*) and lightness.

First priority is always in the elements relaxation, regularity, freedom and contact. Each phase contains the elements of the Training Tree. To create the elements, we should, in our daily training, use the appropriate movements.

Now, what is an appropriate movement? The movement is appropriate when the horse, according to his mental and physical development, is ready for it.

If you remember, we used the example of building a house at the very beginning of this book. We must always start with a solid foundation and build up systematically.

We proceed the same way in training. There are movements appropriate for Phase A, Phase B and Phase C. The quality of the work at Phase B depends on the quality of Phase A, and the quality of the work at Phase C depends on the quality of Phase B.

There is no shortcut without endangering the whole building. Working on Phase C movements before the ones of Phase A are confirmed and the movements of Phase B are sufficiently developed would be like building the roof before the basement.

Unfortunately many riders labour inappropriately on movements the horse is not ready for. They are violating the rules of the Training Tree. Often, they blame the horse for getting tense and resistant when, in fact,

it is the rider´s poor horsemanship that has created the problem.

For example, working on flying changes unless the horse is straight and balanced leads to confusion and tension. On the other hand, once the horse is confirmed in these elements, the flying change comes like a ripe fruit falling from the tree.

The following table is a guide that may help you choose the right exercises and movements for successful training.

In using these movements the way they are recommended, we build the horse´s potential phase by phase. Following a programme that is consistent with the one outlined in the table will diminish the chance for serious mistakes and increase the chance for a sound and happy horse!

In training, we never push the horse to his limit. Many highly talented prospects, especially good jumpers, ended their careers before they even matured for this very reason. We should be satisfied with a slow and steady progress, thus exercising good *horsemanship*. The horse appreciates this and will go that extra mile when absolutely necessary.

GUIDE FOR EXERCISES ACCORDING TO THE *TRAINING TREE*

Appropriate Exercises (not necessarily in this order)	*Why*
Phase A on the Way to Training Level	
• Free walk, trot, canter on straight lines with long rein. • Working paces on a long rein. Circles, turns, figure eights (20m and 15m). Shallow loops at trot, changing rein in all directions. Appropriate lateral bending. • Stretching the topline, showing the horse "the way to the ground". • Trotting poles, cavalletti. Free jumping, hacking cross-country. • Leg yield at walk, turn on the forehand from walk. • Transitions: walk-trot-walk and trot-canter-trot. • No sitting trot unless the horse gives the back.	• Accustom the horse to the rider´s weight. • Strengthen the back muscles. • Horse learns to be a backmover and gives in the back, which becomes relaxed and swinging. • Develop relaxation (1), regularity (2), and freedom (3) in all gaits. • Horse learns the meaning of the forward driving aids and finds first contact with the rider´s hands. • Confirm relationship and confidence.
Phase B on the Way to First Level	
In addition to Phase A: • Lengthenings at walk, trot and canter. On the bit, first half-halts. • Circles, turns, figure eights, corners (10m to 15m). • Positioning and appropriate bending, serpentines. • Leg yield at trot (rail to rail), turn on the forehand from halt to halt. Shoulder fore, simple lead changes in canter through trot. • Quarter turn on the haunches from halt to halt (90 degrees). • Decreasing and increasing the circle. Shallow loop at canter. • Walk-canter transitions. Rein back (one horse length). • Free jumping and first jumps under the rider.	• Confirm Elements 1–3. • Confirm contact. • Horse becomes more submissive and on the aids (5), prerequisite for work on straightness (6), balance (7), Durchlässigkeit (8), and Schwung (9). • Horse develops a First Level frame.

Appropriate Exercises (not necessarily in this order)	Why
Phase C on the Way to Second Level	
In addition to Phase B: • Medium and collected paces in trot and canter (no collected walk yet!). • Improving half-halts and full square halts. • Turns, corners and voltes (8m) in trot and canter. • Appropriate lateral bending. Improved riding in position. • Counter canter. Walk-canter transitions. • Shoulder fore (developing gradually into shoulder-in, prerequisite for later travers and renvers) • Half-turn on the haunches in walk (180 degrees). • Simple lead changes through walk. Rein back (a certain number of steps). • Appropriate cavalletti work. Jumping course of 3-foot fences.	• Confirm Elements 4–7. Rider must create more elevation, carriage, and lightness as well as more lateral flexibility and accuracy. • Work on Durchlässigkeit (8). • Work on Schwung (9). • Work on collection (10). • Horse develops Second Level frame and is ready to proceed towards special training according to his talent for dressage, jumping or eventing.

The above table doesn´t mean that there is intensive training every day. Once in a while, the horse may need one or more days off in the pasture. After a longer period of hard work (show season, for example), he deserves some weeks of vacation. Being turned out between the daily sessions is better for the horse´s mind than for it to be in the stall for 23 hours.

The table is a guideline for the training. It helps us to set up limited training programmes which, according to the training of the horse, should always cover the various elements of *basic training*. It reminds us that *basic training* is an all-around, comprehensive training with all its variations.

Like the school figures recommended in the previous chapter, dressage movements have no end in themselves. We use them in daily training to create the basic elements and to improve the horse´s capability for the next levels.

It is important to understand why the appropriate use of movements is so necessary. The horse cannot go to a physio therapist to work out his problems. He must depend on you to help create suppleness in his body with your knowledge of what the various movements accomplish.

Understand that each of the movements discussed works on muscle groups. By using them in a disciplined way, you help ensure that your horse will remain healthy and willing to work. It is logical that you will need to work the movements on both sides of the horse. If the horse exhibits a weakness or tension on either side, it is a common mistake to avoid that side because it is more difficult for the rider. You must avoid this trap, or you will make the problem worse.

Movements that are useful on one hand are not necessarily useful on the other hand. For example, if your horse bends to the right without a problem but has a hard time bending to the left, you must spend more time riding movements that ask the horse to bend to the left. Remember that straightness is achieved once the horse is equally flexible on both sides.

Another important factor in the use of the movements is to understand that the execution of the movement should never be applied at the expense of the purity of the gaits. Forcing a horse into the movement that it cannot do fluidly defeats the purpose of these exercises. Return to confirm relaxation and regularity until the horse is willing to respond. By easing the horse into what you want him to do, you continue to build, rather than destroy his confidence and his willingness to co-operate.

We must proceed carefully when introducing a new movement to the horse. The horse must *understand* what we are asking for. At first, we should be satisfied with a minimum in the right direction. We let the horse feel our satisfaction and give him a break. The more time we take for a perfect execution, the more the horse will stay relaxed and co-operative.

This principle we also should take to heart for all upper-level movements. It will preserve us from tension, unevenness, tilted necks, "bad mouths", or other creations of poor riding.

While executing a movement, the judge evaluates the quality of the elements involved. If one of the expected elements is lacking or incompletely developed, the whole movement cannot be *sufficient*.

In summary, it must be emphasized that the purpose of these movements is not to prove that you can do them. They are designed to develop the capability of the horse. Each level prepares the horse to go on to develop at a higher level of athletic ability.

At the beginning of this book I mentioned François Robichon de la Guérinière's important claim that the object of dressage is to train the horse so that he is "pleasurable to ride". Let me conclude with a quotation from Gustav Steinbrecht, whose "ride your horse forwards and straighten him" became famous for generations to come. In his famous book, *Gymnasium of the Horse*, he said: "The rider has achieved his aim fully and trained his horse when both forces of the hindquarters – the propulsive force and the carrying power – coupled with elasticity, are fully developed

Fig. 54 By the end of the basic training the fundamental elements of dressage are established. The movement of the horse is relaxed, regular and free, demonstrating straightness, self-carriage and lightness. Shown here is the author with the Trakehnerstallion Hornist. Photo by Henriette von Dallwitz

and when the rider can use and balance the effect of these exactly."

Let us keep this quotation in mind during the special training on our way to the advanced levels.

The training of the young horse is a fascinating experience. It is a wonderful challenge to study his special personality, the way he thinks and feels, and to establish a first relationship. Young horses often are insecure, suspicious, or afraid for some reason. They need your help and patience to become accustomed to the new environment and their new duties. A good relationship makes all handling easier and leads to confidence, willingness, and finally co-operation.

I like the axiom from schooling Western horses: "Make the wrong things difficult and uncomfortable, and make the right things easy and pleasurable."

This is a fundamental wisdom of horsemanship that should be considered as one of the principles for the all-around basic training.

Once you have found your horse´s strong and weak points, his keenness and his talent, you may consider designing a custom-made strategy for his training. *The Elements of Dressage* will help you do this. Follow the logical procedure of the Training tree. This is a reliable guide that represents the safest way to build a solid foundation for the more difficult work to come.

Before finishing this chapter let me say something about freestyle competitions. Freestyle is a wonderful way to express your horse´s personality and demonstrate his capability *within the level he is confirmed in*. A good Third Level demonstration can be very pleasing to watch, while a poorly executed Grand Prix presentation can be ridiculous.

Accuracy in riding the figures and movements must remain a prerequisite for the freestyle. Then, and only then, can freestyle riding become an art.

THE HANGBAHN
THE INCLINED RIDING ARENA

"Horses are honest. They tell us the truth about our riding whether we like it or not."

Occasionally we hear terms like "the nature of the horse", "the natural frame", "natural carriage" or "natural method". What is frequently overlooked, however, is the sensible help nature offers, with its varying terrain, to solve problems during training. While I do not like to sound too repetitious, I must mention again that the goal of dressage is not to teach tricks but to maintain, cultivate and improve the horse´s natural movements under the weight of the rider.

We know that basic training as outlined in the Training tree is an all-around training. Besides the most important work on the flat, we also work over cavalletti or small fences and we go hacking cross-country.

An additional training aid is the **Hangbahn**, a German term that means "sloped arena". In contrast to the wavy track that is helpful to eventers, the training value of the inclined arena is much more effective since it allows continued systematic training.

The idea of the **Hangbahn** was developed in order to help riders who lose influence and whose horses do not stay in front of the leg in the downhill canter. The speed then increases and if there is a jump, it becomes a dangerous situation. In desperation the rider sometimes resorts to the "hand-brake", which creates a stressful fight and makes the horse resistant.

Any horse, especially the event horse, should be able to canter firmly on the rider´s aids no matter whether the horse is moving uphill, downhill, or on the flat. This is a matter of balance and the constantly changing point of gravity, and thus an important goal of the training programme. Working on the sloped arena is valuable not only for cross-country horses but generally for every horse meant to become an athlete. Thus the sloped arena is helpful for the dressage prospect as well. Horses that have learned to overflex and tense up through wrongly interpreted "dressage" work can often achieve the desired suppleness on the sloped arena.

What does a sloped arena look like?

The arena has a slope of no more than 8–12 degrees (*see* Fig. 55). There are two horizontal long sides (60 to 80 metres) and two inclining short sides (30 to 40 metres). The corners are generously rounded. There are prepared tracks for the change of rein. Except

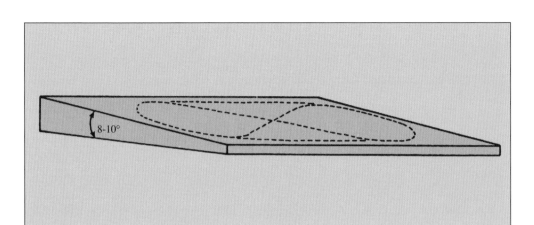

Fig. 55: The Hangbahn, chematic depiction

in really flat areas, one should be able to find sloping ground to establish such an arena more or less close to the ideal plan. Of great importance is the training value created by the change of horizontal lines with slight increases and decreases on bent lines. There are possibilities of riding all the basic school figures like circles, half-circles, voltes and diagonals.

One should be able to view the entire arena from one particular spot so horse and rider can be observed by the trainer or a video camera. Videotaping can be very helpful in this case, especially if it includes comments from the trainer.

Everybody knows riding on trails is not only fun for horse and rider, but instructive as well. Unfortunately, this very important aspect of training often does not get enough attention. Riding outside the regular arena takes more time, and the busy, successful trainer thinks he or she cannot spare it. So the trainer prefers to stay in the indoor arena, where the groom brings him one horse after the other. This, while more economical, is very sad. A sloped arena near the indoor arena can make all the difference. The trainer can plan a "trail day" once or twice a week and take horses out on the sloped arena to do special gymnastic exercises to loosen the physical and mental tension created by the indoor arena routine.

On the sloped arena we follow the same principles as in all other training – from easy work to more difficult tasks. Only if the horse masters the easy work can one increase the demands. A horse that is timid or excited because of balance problems or is not yet strong enough will resist.

Accomplishments, however, can only be achieved when the horse is physically and mentally relaxed and ready to learn. This is the condition required for every co-operation offered by the horse.

We start with walk on the long rein. The horse moves in a relaxed medium walk. The neck is forward and downward with the back muscles relaxed, allowing for a clean walk. The rider should shorten the stirrups two or three holes and sit in a light seat following the movement with the lower-leg contact. The hands follow the motion of the horse´s neck and maintain steady, light contact with the mouth. It is important that the horse learns to move in balance, adjusting constantly to the terrain. In doing so, he learns with ease to shift his point of gravity, no matter whether he is going uphill or downhill. Corrections like *more driving seat or more leg* are superfluous because the nature of the slope causes the horse to give his back or engage the haunches. The rider only needs to follow the movement, thus making the work easier for the horse.

The systematic training on the slope, with its change between stretching (going uphill) and gathering (going downhill), causes the horse to constantly change his point of gravity, alternating the work of the haunches pushing and engaging (and stepping more under). This accordion effect loosens all tension in the back and neck after a while and leads to the desired suppleness.

It is interesting to note that horses almost regularly snort when they are stretching uphill. In the beginning many horses will jig with their heads up going uphill and fall on the forehand going downhill. The sensitive rider will know how to prevent this and teach the horse a more comfortable way. After a while, the horse should stay in a steady four-beat rhythm, absolutely independent of the place: uphill, extended walk; horizontal, medium walk; downhill, collected walk (a basic requirement of dressage). The goal of this training is that the horse slows down and engages by himself as soon as he goes downhill. The independent engagement going downhill is the most important criteria when working on the slope. It is the leading goal in trot and canter work as well. The rider´s hand is hardly active at all.

Before starting with trot work, the walk has to be confirmed. The horse should have found a stable connection. Ride occasional halts, especially downhill. It helps the balance. We do not have to elaborate on the trot work because it follows the same principles as the walk. We want to establish a working trot with rhythm, allowing a lengthening of a stride uphill (stretching) and expecting a gathering (engagement) downhill.

A swinging back and soft topline are important goals. The horse is on the bit and on command should enjoy chewing the reins out of the rider´s hand (especially going uphill).

In canter we follow the same principles. When the trot is accomplished, we work in canter. Canter work is the most effective but also the most difficult work on the slope. The muscles of the back and of the haunches are involved a great deal, because downhill, the hind legs have to jump well under. To avoid unnecessary excitement, only a short canter is advised.

If after four to five training sessions, the horse is able to canter in rhythm quietly and regularly on both leads uphill (lengthening the canter stride) and downhill (collecting the canter stride), then both the horse and rider did good work.

The dressage horse, possibl sour from too much arena work, awakens to new liveliness. It makes it easier for him to engage and stay in balance, because of the uneven track he has to deal with. For cross-country horses who know this type of work, one can add poles or cavalletti on the slope.

In most cases this will not cause problems because the horses are in balance and know their job. Horses and riders who are prepared this way will be in good condition and have an easier time on cross-country courses. The "handbrake stuggle" described earlier can thus be avoided.

TRANSITIONS

THE TUNING AND TIMING OF THE AIDS

"The rider thinks – the horse executes." Alois Podhajsky

Transitions are highly valued in dressage tests. They can prove that the horse is durchlässig, one of the fundamental elements of basic training. That's why in the Collective Remarks of dressage tests, **Durchlässigkeit** is multiplied by a coefficient of 2. Before dealing with this subject, let me recall some facts mentioned in previous chapters. The US *Equestrian Rule Book* says that "Suppleness (*Durchlässigkeit*) is the physical ability of the horse to shift the point of equilibrium smoothly forward and back as well as laterally without stiffness or restistance. Suppleness is manifested by the horse´s fluid response to the legs and seat. Suppleness is best judged in transitions."

Durchlässigkeit is a prerequisite for a quality half-halt. It allows the energy created by the driving aids to flow through the horse´s body up to the mouth. The rider receives the forward propelling energy in his hands and transmits it back to the haunches, which makes the horse step more under the body, which in turn improves straightness and balance. By half-halts we prepare and execute transitions. The response to the half-halt determines the quality of the transition. That

is why in training, frequent transitions are most helpful for developing **Schwung** and collection.

Since **Durchlässigkeit** is best judged in transitions, quite a lot of them are asked for in dressage tests. No matter at what level, all transitions must be soft, flowing, in contact, in balance, and without tension or irregularity. The aids must be distinct, though effortless and almost invisible. The horse should appear to perform of his own accord.

How to Achieve a Correct Transition

Towards the end of basic training, the horse travels in a way that is relaxed, regular, and ground-covering. He is on the aids, responding willingly to signals from the seat, legs and reins. He is sufficiently straightened and balanced. As a result of this preparation, the horse will respond to half-halts, which makes him ready for the work on transitions. There is often significant difference in the quality of transitions. Sometimes a transition is good, and other times it is bad, even when the rider is sure the aids have been the same.

What is the reason for this difference? The answer is the *timing of the aids*. We know that the aids must be co-ordinated with the horse´s motion. This way they can help the horse in executing the movement. Correct timing of the aids especially facilitates transitions of all kinds, enabling the horse to move under the weight of the rider as it does in nature.

There are riders who work very hard on dressage without much of a chance of success. They often get frustrated and blame the horse for it. In almost all of these cases it is not the horse, it is the rider who is causing the problem. A poor seat cannot follow or support the motion. As a result, the aids cannot be effective. The rider permanently bothers the horse by not sitting *in* the horse and by not being able to control the aids. The horse responds to this awkwardness by labouring and becoming shortgaited and stiff. Here only an experienced trainer can help. After fixing the position and application of the aids the rider must learn to feel and to co-operate with the motion of the horse. *We want to ride with the horse, not against the horse.*

In order to co-ordinate and later tune the aids, it is necessary to know how the horse moves, especially how and in what sequence the horse sets his legs in the different gaits. Everyone can learn this by observing and studying the gaits on horses moving at liberty and under the rider. Videotapes in slow motion are most instructive. Mirrors are also helpful. Knowing the patterns of the legs and feet in theory will help you access the feel from the saddle.

There are transitions *within* a gait (to shorten or lengthen a stride) and transitions *from one gait to another*, including rein back and halt. For any transition the horse must be prepared with half-halts. The horse must be balanced and in front of the legs. The quality of the transition itself depends on the co-ordination of the aids with the motion of the horse, or in other words, the timing.

Transitions within a gait seem simple. They are! As long as the horse is connected from behind onto the bit, and thus **durchlässig**, he can use his back properly and stay regular and in rhythm. For lengthening or shortening the strides, the activity of the haunches is most important. In both cases the rider applies the half-halts, asking with the legs for the horse to step more energetically under the body, especially in shortening the strides. The rider´s legs co-operate with the horse´s hind legs. The right leg with the right hind, the left leg with the left hind. The signal from the leg must happen the very moment the hind is about to strike off the ground. In this phase only the horse responds instantaneously. Once the rider knows how to apply the aids this way with the horse´s motion, the rider will find that the horse becomes more responsive and more willing to work. Riders who lack this feel for timing usually waste energy by acting against the motion.

As mentioned before, everyone can learn the timing of the aids. It requires a feel for regularity and rhythm. Riders with musical talent will learn more easily than those without. The leg yield at the walk is the best movement for teaching the timing of the aids. The rider should get used to counting the steps. First the right hind, then the left. Later alternatively, left, right, left, right. The signals from the legs should not be visible. The connected horse maintains contact with the rider´s hand. The reins are straightened and the hands are following the motion. With half-halts we close and release the hand, making sure we don´t irritate the horse with bad timing.

The tuning of the rein aids with the motion of the horse is more difficult than it may seem. But here is the key for the timing: the hand is part of the horse´s mouth and should be soft but steady in contact. For both downward and upward transitions we need seat and leg aids. The hand closes for shortening and releases for lengthening the strides without losing contact.

Transitions from one gait to another require more skill from the rider. The reason for this is obvious: both pace and rhythm change. Transition from walk to trot, the easier transition, is already a challenge to fine-tune the aids. The rider feels the movement and the horse must move energetically forward, the two diagonal legs stepping well under the horse´s body. The transition from trot to walk must also be prepared with a half-halt, causing the back legs to step well under the body to act as "brakes". In all transitions the purity of the rhythm and the regularity of the gaits are of first priority.

Let us take a look at the walk-canter transition. Here the correct timing plays an important role. The horse transitions from a four-beat gait (walk) to a three-beat gait (canter). In order to start the canter at a very special moment. We need an impeccable feel for the motion and for the timing of the aids. The canter starts with the outside hind (first beat), followed by the inside hind and the outside fore (second beat), followed by the inside fore (third beat). The procedure is as follows: half-halts for getting the horse to listen, positioning the horse for the canter and waiting for the inside hind to take the weight for releasing the canter. This is the only way to start the canter correctly. If we miss the right moment for the release, the horse cannot start the canter instantly, but would need a few trot steps before picking it up. Quite often we observe this bad timing in dressage tests and wonder how the rider could get a 6 on "application of the aids".

The best way to learn timing is on an old schoolmaster. He knows the job and teaches patiently. But schooling the eye by watching other riders also helps a lot in developing the knowledge about the horse´s motion and the feel for timing. The timing is of utmost importance in flying changes.

The canter-walk transition must also be sufficiently prepared for with half-halts. This works best at a certain phase, that is at the second beat of the canter when the diagonal feet are about to hit the ground. These two legs of the horse can act like brakes at the same time. If we miss this phase, the horse needs additional effort to maintain balance, which prevents the transition from having a harmonious appearance.

Logically the canter-trot transition works the same way. Observing the horse in freedom we can see the horse doing so on his own and we can learn that good timing is *allowing* the movement, rather than asking for it. Simple lead changes through trot or through walk are First and Second Level movements.

Here also, in addition to straightness, balance, and **Durchlässigkeit**, precise timing makes all the difference in the scores. Correct simple changes through walk on a straight line are indispensible for teaching the flying changes later. As soon as the horse learns to go from canter into walk without losing balance and then the canter straight from walk, the flying change should give no problems – it is all about timing! For this reason, the Prix St. James asks for simple changes on the centreline. It is indeed difficult to describe the necessary steps taken at the simple change but I will nevertheless attempt it. Let us assume the transition from canter to walk was successful, then the inside hind (left) is well under the body. While we change the bend to the right, we count three steps of the hind legs: 1 – hind right, 2 – hind left, 3 – hind right. Just before the right hind leg puts weight on, we give the aid to canter right. The right lead canter begins with the outside (left) hind leg. When you miss the moment, you have to wait another four steps before the horse can correctly strike off again.

Transitions from trot to canter or canter to trot should also be harmonious and performed with effortless aids. We know, in trot, the horse swings first the one pair, then the other pair of diagonal legs through; in canter we also have a phase where two diagonal legs are in contact with the ground. This is the most stable phase.

Let us assume we want to canter on the left rein. We have to strike off with the right hind leg (outside). The most natural way for the horse to strike off is when the diagonal pair, inner hind and outer fore, is on the ground. That frees the right to do the first canter step.

For reasons of balance (centrifugal) it is easier to do the trot-canter transition on a circle.

The quality of canter-trot transitions once more depends on the timing. Let us just remind ourselves of the sequence of the canter: 1. outside hind, 2. diagonal inside fore and outside hind, 3. outside hind etc. When the horse can use the diagonal sequence (no. 2) as base for the first step in trot, you will have harmonious and natural transition.In closing let me point out that with correct timing of the aids, we improve the harmony between the horse and rider remarkably. Since we don´t ride *against* the horse, but are with the horse, we are no burden for him. Rather, we *help him* use his body like in nature.

Everyone can learn this, which is nothing but co-ordinating the aids with the motion of the horse. Prerequisite for successful learning is a good seat and a trainer who knows.

THE PRIX ST. JAMES
A COMBINED DRESSAGE TEST (CDT)

"A horse without a solid foundation in dressage is handicapped for life."

The classical art of riding is a cultural treasure of the old world. To cherish and carry this on is a fascinating task for everybody who carries responsibility in the world of riding.

Officials, judges, and trainers must realize that any deviation from the classical rules of dressage risks destroying this cultural treasure for all time.

The sport of dressage has won many new friends. The number of those who are striving for the higher levels has increased remarkably. Often, however, people do not realize how long this road is and how much patience is required to bring along a talented horse. To fully develop, under the rider, the abilities nature provided to the horse is a long and difficult process.

Today it seems that through "technology" everything is possible. One uses technology to get to the end results easier and faster. Riding, however, is still one of the last oases where technology has not yet found entry – and must never be allowed to do so.

A horse will always be a horse – with all his strong and weak points. The horse´s training must be adjusted to his mental and physical abilities. Force only leads to those sad and often seen results: the horse has "learned" the lesson, but on the way he has lost all the sparkle and charm in his movements. This should *never* be the aim of any training.

Here, the Prix St. James sets a goal. It encourages all ambitious riders to take enough time to develop a solid foundation before showing FEI level. It is designed as the first part of a two part test (the second part is the Prix St. Georges) that evaluates the preparedness of the horse and rider for international competition.

In Part 1, the rider shows Second Level movements demonstrating this foundation, which is a prerequisite for any upper-level horse. In the Collective Remarks, the judge evaluates the quality of the basic elements of dressage, as we know them from the Training tree. The Prix St. James is an important milestone that indicates the readiness of the horse and rider to graduate to working toward the FEI Level.

In my opinion, horses that do not score at least 60 percent in Part 1 do not have the foundation necessary for Part 2, the Prix St. Georges. The combined score for Part 1 and Part 2 is used to determine the winner.

PRIX ST. JAMES
PART I (BASIC TEST)

Purpose: Horses competing in FEI level must have a solid foundation. This test examines the quality of the basic elements (Training Tree). The value of the Collective Remarks is remarkably higher than usual (3:2)

Conditions: Standard arena; Time 7 Minutes; Horse: ordinary snaffle bridle; Rider: short coat, all trot sitting, unless specified otherwise

Maximum points possible: Part I (Basic Test) = 500
                         Part II (Prix St. Georges) = 400
                         Prix St. James total = 900

		Movement	Points possible	Coeff.
1	A-X	Enter working trot		
	X	Halt, salute, proceed working trot		
	C	Track right	10	
2	M-F-K	Working trot	10	
3	K-X-M	Medium trot, rising		
	M	Working trot	10	
4	H	Medium trot		
	E	Cicle left, 20m , once	10	
5	K	Working trot		
	A	Halt, 5 seconds immobility, rein back four steps, Proceed working trot	10	
6	F-X-H	Medium trot		
	H	Working trot	10	
7	B	Circle right, 20m, once, make the horse chew the bit out of the hands	10	2
8	B-F	Take up the reins	10	2
9	F	Collected trot		
	A	Down centreline		
	betw. D & X	Shoulder-in right	10	
10	betw. X & G	Shoulder-in left		
	C	Track left	10	
11	S	Working canter		
	E	Circle left, 20m, once Change legs when while crossing the centreline, proceed working canter	10	

12	A	Down centreline	Points possible	Coeff.
	X	Simple change of lead (through walk)		
	C	Track right, proceed working canter	10	2
13	B	Circle right, 20m, once, change legs while crossing		
		centreline, proceed working canter	10	
14	K-X-M	Medium canter	10	
15	M	Collected canter		
	M-S	Collected counter canter	10	
16	S	Simple change of lead (through walk) proceed collected canter	10	
17	F-X-H	Medium canter	10	
18	H	Collected canter		
	H-R	Collected counter canter	10	
19	R-A	Working trot	10	
20	A	Medium walk		
	K-X-M	Free walk on a long rein	10	2
21	M	Take up the reins		
	C	Collected trot	10	2
22	H-K	Medium trot		
	K	Collected trot	10	
23	A	Down centreline		
	X	Medium walk, reins in one (left) hand	10	
24	G	Halt, Salute	10	2
		Leave arena at a free walk with loose rein at A		

	Technical Part	points possible	240 + 60
		total	300

COLLECTIVE REMARKS:
(Derived from the Basic Elements of the Training Tree)

		Coeff.
Relaxation	*without tension in body and mind, confidence*	20
Regularity	*pure rhythm, pure tempo*	20
Freedom of gaits	*desire to move forwards, natural ease*	20
Contact	*steadiness in accepting rider's hands*	20
Straightness	*travel correctly on one track, ambidexterity*	20
Balance	*lateral and longitudinal equilibrium, lightness*	20
Durchlässigkeit	*suppleness, submissivness, obedience*	20
Schwung	*impulsion, elasticity, cadence, energy*	20
Collection	*engagement of haunches, elevation*	20
Rider's position and application of the aids		20

	Collective Remarks	Points possible	200
	PRIX ST. JAMES, Part I	Points possible total	500

LATERAL MOVEMENTS
WHEN – HOW – WHY

"Lateral movements fulfil their purpose only if correctly ridden."

In basic training our young horse has learned to respond to the rider´s aids. The horse knows the meaning of the sideways pushing leg that is positioned a little behind the girth. And the horse knows the meaning of the controlling outside leg that is positioned one hand further back. The contact with the mouth is confirmed, the horse is straight "in the rails", balanced, and durchlässig. Now it's time to begin with lateral movements.

Lateral movements not only play an important role in the training of the dressage horse, they are useful in training eventers and jumpers, as well. In the same way that all lessons in Training and First to Fourth Level are not an end in themselves, lateral movements too, are solely *means to a goal*. They serve the trainer in honing the application of aids as well as improving rideability. The lateral movements include shoulder-in, travers, renvers and half pass. They are executed in walk (for introduction), trot and canter.

The lateral movements are especially useful in promoting *Durchlässigkeit*, *Schwung* and *collection*. The high gymnastic value of lateral work renders the horse more supple and simultaneously more obedient. As allur-

ing as it may seem, work on the lateral movements should not begin prior to the horse's achievement of a sound foundation as set forth in the Training Tree. As we know, the Training Tree encompasses the ten elements of basic training: 1) relaxation, 2) regularity, 3) freedom, 4) contact, 5) on the aids (responsiveness), 6) straightness, 7) balance, 8) **Durchlässigkeit**, 9) **Schwung**, 10) the beginning of collection.

This degree of maturity and development should be achieved after one-and-a-half to two years of systematic training when the horse has developed the physical and mental capability to move on. Much will be depending on the rider´s skill and tact to maintain the horse´s willingness to co-operate.

The experienced trainer will know when to introduce lateral movements without inflicting any problems. Rushing a horse into lateral movements can only cause setbacks. The remedies for such problems are costly and require much additional time and patience.

If, for example, the elements of the Training Tree have not been developed properly and the horse has not yet found his balance under the rider, it is certain that problems in relaxation, regularity and contact will arise. As a result, tension and stiffness will put an early end to the charm of a young prospect. With this kind of "presentation" judges should not have mercy. After all, they bear responsibility for the purity of the art.

Lateral movements can only be as good as their prerequisite elements of the Training Tree. As soon as one of the elements is shown insufficiently the score for the movement performed cannot be "good". If, for example, in the shoulder-in the lateral bend is insufficient, the score for the shoulder-in should also be "insufficient". That may sound harsh, but it is meant to be! This is the only way we can avoid the superficial success that encourages riders to force movements the horse is not physically or mentally ready for. The horses will in fact be grateful for more horsemanship.

THE SHOULDER-IN:
Mother of All Lateral Movements

Let us presume that the young horse in training has confirmed Elements 1–7 of the Training Tree. In other words, the horse has achieved sufficient straightness (Element 6) and balance (Element 7). It is now time to begin the work on two tracks. In this case, one should not wait any longer since the learning capacity, as is well known, decreases with increasing age.

The straight horse is equally bendable to both sides. He is capable of moving in bal-ance on straight lines and on curved lines. The horse moves in clean regularity and on true contact. Corners (as a sector of an eight-metre volte) are no problem. Prepared in such manner, initial attempts to perform lateral movements ought not to be an issue. After all, the horse is on the aids (Element 5) and soon will learn to respond to the new influences. Short breaks and ample praise are highly recommended for this.

The shoulder-in ought to be the first lateral movement the horse learns. It is easiest for the horse to understand, as it is akin to the already practised leg yield. The shoulder-in and the leg yield are similar only in so far as the horse is moving against its positioning. *In any other way the shoulder-in cannot be compared to the leg yield! The purpose and goal of each movement are fundamentally different.*

Let us compare the different exercises:
The leg yield (Fig. 56a) is a basic exercise to teach horse (and rider) the effect of inside aids. As is well known, the horse is straight with the head positioned to the inside. The horse´s inside legs are stepping in front and across the outer ones. The rider lets the horse *yield* to his left lower *leg*.

This exercise is executed at a medium walk and a working trot and needs to be ridden in good regularity and good contact. It is also an excellent way to teach the rider about the very important timing of the leg aids. Furthermore, the leg yield is a superb exercise to get a horse relaxed (Element 1) and to co-ordinate the aids. As soon, though, as horse and rider cover this exercise in walk and trot, it

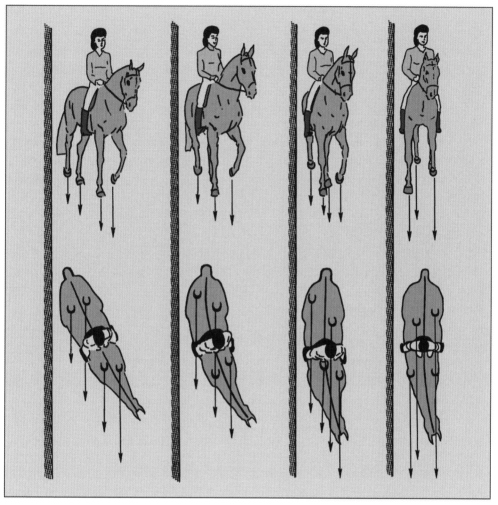

Fig. 56a: Leg-yielding for loosening and fine-tuning the aids, four tracks, legs cross.

Fig. 56b: Shoulder-in improves Durchlässigkeit and Schwung. Lateral bend, three tracks, inside hoof steps under centre of gravity, no "crossing" of legs.

Fig. 56c: Shoulder fore. Useful introduction to shoulder-in. Little lateral bend, four tracks.

Fig. 56d: Riding in position. Straightening effect, three tracks, inside fore on the same line as inside hind.

may be dispensed with and lateral movements may commence.

Note that the leg yield as well as the turn on the forehand is not a lateral movement according to the classical rules. These ask the horse to move the forehand in front of the haunches and do not allow the haunches to "fall out".

The **shoulder-in** (Fig. 56b), on the other hand serves the improvement of *Durchlässigkeit* (Element 8), *Schwung* (Element 9), and *collection* (Element 10). In the shoulder-in, the torso of the horse is no longer straight as with the leg yield, but assumes, appropriate for the state of training, a lateral bending. The high collecting value lies primarily in the fact that the horse no longer is yielding the inside hind leg to the (inside) rider's leg, like in the leg yield, but is asked through lateral bending to place the inside hind leg in front and below the centre of gravity. The inside hind foot is set together with the outside front on one line parallel to the rail (Fig. 56b). This **line of energy** is the base for direction and thrust and plays the decisive role not only in the shoulder-in, but in training for all lateral movements.

In principle, you should never attempt to ride a new movement "correctly" right away. You need to proceed with small steps into the right direction and allow yourself ample time to reflect on your work. This is practising rider´s tact. The longer way is usually the more successful one. Short-cuts lead into cul-de-sacs. That is particularly true for the degree of lateral bending which should be increased with caution. Relaxation, regularity, contact, and later on, Schwung are elements that must not be neglected.

A leg yield-like shoulder-in is as faulty as a shoulder–in-like leg yield.

A good preparatory exercise for shoulder-in is **shoulder fore** (Fig. 56c), which was developed from riding in position (Fig. 56d)

which, in turn, resulted from the work on straightening. Shoulder fore is initially ridden on the long side of the arena and best introduced from a 20-metre circle. The even lateral bending, which is created on the circle line, is maintained on the straight, taking the horses shoulder "fore" to the inside so that the inner hind foot is placed *in the direction between the front feet*. Caution needs to be taken not to have the haunches fall out. The dock of the tail thus remains nearly parallel to the rail.

Any two-track work is only of value if the rider produces the necessary feeling. That is, the rider needs to be capable of sustaining the lateral bending on the straight that had previously been developed on the circle without tightening up which, without fail, would create problems with the horse.

At this time it is helpful to mention the bending seat required here. The bending seat is a minor loading and advancing of the inner seat bone, thus advancing the inner hip slightly; inner leg at the girth (driving); outer leg one hand back (guarding); outer shoulder slightly forward. Thus the principle of two parallels is preserved as the horse bends: the rider's shoulder like horses shoulder, rider's hip like horses hip (Fig. 57). Here the rider's head should follow the direction of the horses head. The outside rein conveys direction and carriage, the inside rein attends to position and softness of contact. The bending seat often causes difficulties for the rider since it calls for a minor twist in the torso. So this should not be honed *before the dressage seat*

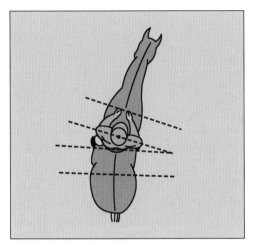 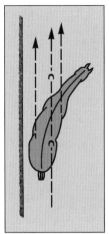 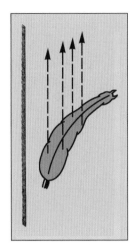

Fig 57: The bending seat. Hips and shoulders of rider parallel to hips and shoulders of horse.

Fig 58: Shoulder-in right
a) Correct – Three tracks: inside hind and outside fore form a line of energy.
b) Wrong – Four tracks: producing a leg-yield slike shoulder-in.

is established and the rider´s aids independently, otherwise a collapsed hip, raised knees, stiff upper body, and pulling on the reins will ensue. Such habits can be corrected later, but only with great difficulty.

Aids for lateral movement are satisfactorily discussed in many riding manuals, so we will not discuss that subject any further. But let me finally stress the importance of the outer leg as bending leg and the inner leg as a cornerstone or bending pivot.

The willing cooperation of the horse tells us that we are on the right track. Yet each training sessions calls for a reconfirmation of the elements of the TRAINING TREE before we may commence work on shoulder-in and, if appropriate, increase the demands. The main concern here is the "taking-in" of the shoulder without allowing the haunches to fall out or impairing the impulsion. The rail is initially a helpful guide for this *increased bending of the ribcage*. As soon as the haunches fall out, the tailbone is no longer parallel to the rail. If the horse´s tailbone is not parallel to the wall, we know that the horse is no longer placing the inner hindleg forwards *and under the centre of gravity* but crossing (as in the leg yield). This obstructs the effort to collect, thus rendering the exercise useless, if not counterproductive. The result is nothing but eyewash for the uninitiated who have no understanding of the meaning of shoulder-in and admire the "crossing" as a higher level of the art (Fig. 58b). This widely spread misconception will be dealt with in the discussions of travers, renvers and half-pass.

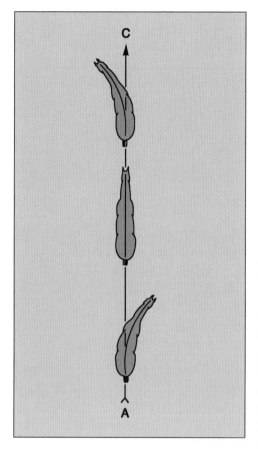

C

A

Fig 59: Shoulder-in on the centreline. Notice that the hindquarters remain on the centre when the shoulder-in changes hand.

The old masters referred to the shoulder-in as the "mother of all lateral movements". If that is so – and there is no doubt about it – the volte is the "grandmother" and the circle the "great-grandmother". The lateral bending necessary for the shoulder-in is really the result of an accurate volte, which, in turn, is made possible by systematic work on the circle.

Like any lateral movement, the shoulder-in is developed from a curved line where the established lateral bending must be maintained in the lessons on the straight or the bend. To make it easier for the horse (using a rider´s tact) one might want to start off on a circle (10–15-metre) to make sure that the horse is adapting to the arc from poll to tail without falling out with either the forehand or the haunches.

The horse will, perhaps, adapt effortlessly to the arc on one side while on the other side resistance might be encountered, caused by the natural crookedness.

This obvious lack of straightness (Element 6) ought to have been addressed prior to serious work on shoulder-in. Only too quickly problems may creep up here, so be sure to confirm prerequisite elements. As a matter of principle, lateral movements including shoulder-in should be mirror-image on either hand. Bending (straightness), contact, regularity, relaxation and impulsion should be consistent on both sides. Deviations indicate flaws in the basic training, and should be a first priority. A score of 7 on one hand and a 4 on the other hand are a clear giveaway. A rather revealing exercise in this case is an alternating shoulder-in along the centreline where the forehand is taken left and right without letting the haunches leave the centreline. In other words the tail is on the centreline (Fig. 59). This movement is asked for in the Prix St. James, Part 1, in order to test the horse´s ambidexterity.

Only after the symmetry on both hands has been established, demands may be increased:

shoulder-in on a circle, counter shoulder-in, and added lateral bending and collection. However, let us not forget: as soon as one of the elements of basic training is adversely affected, the demands need to be reduced.

TRAVERS

We approach teaching the travers (haunches-in) in the same manner as the shoulder-in. We initiate the exercise from a 10-metre circle with appropriate lateral bending and lead the horse onto the straight along the rail, maintaining the bend. As the shoulder is brought to the inside in the shoulder-in, the croup is brought to the inside in the travers, a task mainly assigned to the outer leg, which keeps the haunches slightly off the track.

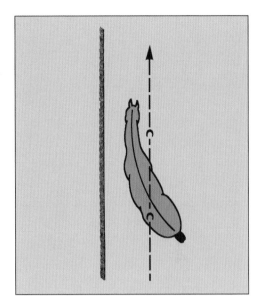

Fig. 60: In travers right, the left hind and right fore form the line of energy, which enhances thrust and Schwung, the prerequisite for collection.

While at the shoulder-in the inside hind leg was called upon increasingly to step under, at the travers the *outside hind-leg* is now expected to do the same.

Initially we are satisfied with a light bending (set-off of the haunches from the rail) since we do not want to impair the elements of the basic training in the TRAINING TREE. It may well take several weeks until – like with shoulder-in – the lateral bending may be increased to an 8m bend without resistance when schooling the travers. Here the horse places the outer hind leg *forwards and under the centre of gravity* while it sets the diagonal fore on the line of energy, which runs parallel to the rail (Fig. 60). A comparison with the criteria of shoulder-in is re-

commended. Crossing the legs makes the horse move on four tracks, which may increase the loosening effect of the exercise. But there is a warning: a lot of stifle problems in dressage horses result from asking too much of this kind of work.

The degree of bend – and therefore the setting-off of the hind off the rail – *needs to allow the horse at any time to effortlessly look into the direction of the movement* (Fig. 60). This is a principle that – even at advanced levels – is too frequently violated and needs to be addressed under the subject of the half-pass.

Transitions from travers to shoulder-in and shoulder-in to travers, with or without a volte, are excellent exercises to help riders and horses

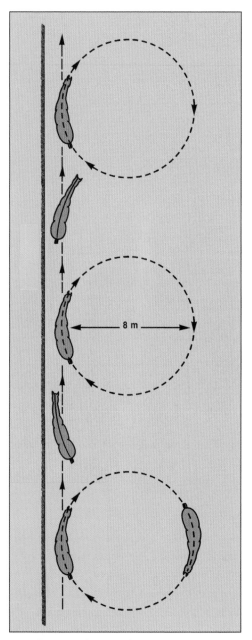

Fig. 61: The eight-metre lateral bend stays in the shoulder-in – travers transitions. The line of energy changes from the left diagonal (travers) to the right diagonal (shoulder-in) to the left diagonal.

understand the interrelationship of these movements (Fig. 61). High gymnastic value is also to be attributed to transitions from travers to counter shoulder-in and back to travers (Fig. 62) since the line of energy, that is the line of the left hind and the right fore, remains the same despite the alternating lateral bending, thus making strong demands on the balance.

Like shoulder-in, travers can be ridden on any straight or curved line without the support of the rail. *Decreasing and increasing the circle* is also well suited to school balance and the stepping-under of the haunches. Here the degree of difficulty is increased, but should be limited when the horse begins to labour. In the forefront of all considerations, for sure, is the horse´s well-being, the maintenance of his original charm, and his desire for achievement.

RENVERS

The opposite movement to the travers is the renvers. It is related to the travers just as the shoulder-in is related to the counter shoulder-in. In the renvers left, the horse moves on the right lead in bending left, the hind on the track (along the rail), the fore led into the arena. Here too (as with travers), the horse places the outer (right) hind *under the centre of gravity* while the diagonal (inside) fore is placed on the **line of energy**, parallel to the rail (Fig. 63). Later on, when working with more lateral bend, the horse will be moving on four tracks and is necessarily crossing the legs. This shows that renvers is the same exercise as travers, only demands on the horse are greater on curved lines, similar to counter shoulder-in and shoulder-in. It ought to be understandable that these counter lessons should only be approached after basic movements have been well established on both leads.

Many a rider, who is introduced to lateral movements, find it difficult to understand that travers and renvers are really the same exercise. That becomes more obvious when the movement is ridden without the rail, for example, along the centreline. Then it is merely a question of wether the horse is led along centreline with the forehand (travers) or the haunches (renvers). Direction, positioning and bending are absolutely equal (Fig. 64).

This does not change on curved lines which, as previously mentioned, make higher demands on horse and rider. Figure 64 also shows how travers and renvers are introduced on centreline. While the horse moves in a travers in direction of its bending on the centreline (imaginary rail), it *crosses* this line in a renvers and travels in the same manner on the *other side* of the line. Horses have no problem with differentiating the two movements, some riders, however, find it confusing.

The renvers may also be developed out of the shoulder-in (Fig. 65). Here the transitions from shoulder-in to renvers to shoulder-in to renvers are of high gymnastic value. The hindquarters always stay on the track. Although the lateral bending changes here, the line of energy stays the same (right hind

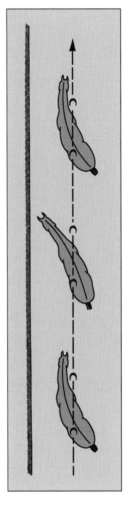

Fig. 62: In the travers counter shoulder-in transition the line of energy (left diagonal) does not change (left diagonal).

Fig. 63: Renvers left is the counter of travers right line of energy.

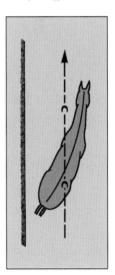

and left fore). The right hind works in one case as the inside leg (shoulder-in) and in the other as the outside (renvers).

Another instructive exercise is the short-turn in renvers (Fig. 66), where the horse is turning on the haunches. This turn should be introduced to the horse at a collected walk The outside hind always steps forwards and under the centre of gravity.

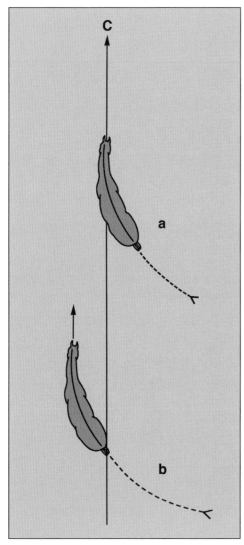

Fig. 64: Developing travers (a) and renvers (b) on centreline.

HALF-PASS

Once the shoulder-in and the travers – with and without the support of the rail – no longer create a problem, the horse is ready for the half-pass. Well-ridden half-passes are not only pretty to look at but give evidence of the quality of the elements achieved in theTraining Tree. The horse must be balanced (Element 7) and durchlässig (Element 8) which is indispensable for developing Schwung (Element 9) and collection (Element 10). Once familiar with that model everybody will understand that this is not possible without a solid foundation of the Elements 1–6. Violations of the Training Tree concept always leave their imprint, be that on the joints, the back, the poll or the mouth.

Once we can ride the travers, the half-pass won't be a problem. Both the movements, as a matter of fact, are congruent in purpose and means. Yet, some riders have difficulties here in perception. In order to remedy this, one should initially not think of half-pass but only of a correct travers along a diagonal *line of movement*. That is the half-pass (Fig. 67). The diagonal line functions as the imaginary rail, and we do know how to ride a travers along a rail. The horse moves in the direction of its bending forwards and sideways and on three tracks. The head points in the direction of movement. The tailbone stays almost parallel to the long side. Once the angle of movement increases in more advanced work, the horse needs more lateral bend and starts moving on four tracks. Later, transitions are very educational – shoulder-in to travers to shoulder-in (Fig. 69). In this exercise a volte could be added at any time.

This way the rider is developing the feeling that all lateral movements are dependent on the correctness of the volte and closely related to each other. Only if this perception prevails can the work with lateral movements lead to the desired success.

As is evident, with the necessary equestrian skill, there are a number of ways to make use of lateral movements to improve rideability. One only needs to be aware of a few points:
• Is the horse truly secure in its basic training (Training Tree)?
• Which lateral movement would be really useful right now ?
• What do I want to improve (balance, *Durchlässigkeit, Schwung,* collection)?
• Which direction has to be worked on in order to counteract rather than aggravate the horse´s natural crookedness?
• What pace is the most appropriate?

If the work on lateral movements produces no improvement in the rideability, but instead new problems arise, you should abandon the work and happily ride straight ahead on *one track*. The advice of an expert may help.

Working on lateral movements means in the first place moving *forwards*. The *sideways* movement is merely an outcome of the lateral bend. In order to establish that forward feeling, just think of leading the forehand in front of you, like at the shoulder-in (Fig. 69) and keep the haunches under control and in the rails. This way you develop the utmost propulsion from the haunches (line of energy).

Like with the introduction of any new movement, we start by making the half-pass easy before gradually making it more difficult. Decisive for that is the relaxed and will-

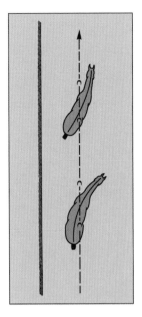

Fig. 65: In the transition from shoulder-in to renvers to shoulder-in, the line of energy does not change.

Fig. 66: Short-turn in renvers in walk from shoulder-in. Unchangeable, clear, four-beat. Higher degree of Durchlässigkeit.

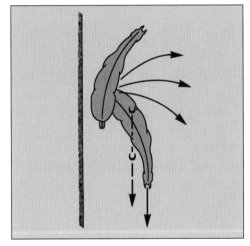

ing co-operation of the horse. But what now is easy, difficult, and just unreasonable? In order to be able to judge this, let's look at the large standard arena 60 by 20 metres (see Fig. 70a).

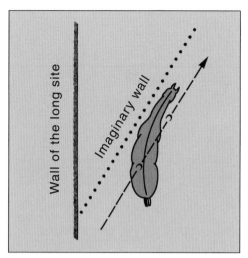

Fig. 67: The half-pass
Head in the direction of movement and tailbone nearly
parallel to rail gives the desired lateral bend. That way
the line of energy is effective.

Crossing the arena there are various connecting lines. Let's take point K to start. From here begin the following lines of movement for a half pass right: K–G, K–M, K–R, K–B, K–P.

The difficulty of the half-pass is determined by the angle of the line of movement to the rail (angle of movement). The more obtuse the angle, the more demanding the half-pass. The demand ends when the horse begins to labour – when relaxation, regularity, contact or *Schwung* is beginning to get lost.

At a half-pass *two criteria on every line of movement need* to be secure. First, the horse should effortlessly look into the line of movement, and secondly, the horse´s tail should stay nearly parallel to the rail (as with shoulder-in, *see* Fig. 69). To achieve these two criteria the rider must ensure a *clean lateral*

bending that corresponds to the line of movement and enables the horse to optimally convert the thrust of the haunches into *Schwung*. Therefore it can be deduced that any deviation from the line of energy inevitably brings about a reduction in thrust and impulsion.

The physically possible angle of movement is, consequently, determined by the extent of the lateral bending that the horse is capable of maintaining throughout the exercise. The degree differs according to the level of training. Since the ability for lateral bending is developed on circles and voltes, a scale can be inferred: a ten-metre bend is the lateral bending that corresponds to a ten-metre circle; an eight-metre bend corresponds to an eight-metre volte, and so on.

Let us take a look at Figure 70b. This depicts why at a larger angle of movement the demands on lateral bending need to be increased (in order to satisfy the two criteria).

The easiest version of the half-pass (for introduction) is the line of movement K–G, which calls for a 20-metre circle bend; K–M demands a ten-metre circle bend; K–R an eight-metre circle bend; and K–B a six-metre circle bend.

We know that at Third Level the half-pass calls for an angle of movement of about 30 degrees. This asks for an eight-metre circle bend. At Fourth Level it can be up to 40 degrees, which is a six-metre circle bend and the maximum bend that a fully trained dressage horse is capable of producing. That means that according to the two criteria, the line of movement K–B is the shortest diagonal on which, in a 20 x 60 arena, a half-pass may be ridden.

Fig. 68: Half-pass right in Grand Prix. The horse in optimum lateral bend, moving in the direction of his head
"forwards". Line of energy effective. Isabell Werth on
Antony FRH.

pass or not, miss the point of the issue. At the
half-pass it is the *correct lateral bend* that the
horse maintains along the line of movement,
without violating the two criteria of the half-
pass: *Head positioned into direction of movement, tail nearly parallel to the long side of
the arena.*

Fig. 69: Shoulder-in – half-pass – shoulder-in.
Transitions of high training value
Line of energy changes but the lateral bend and neck bend
stay the same.

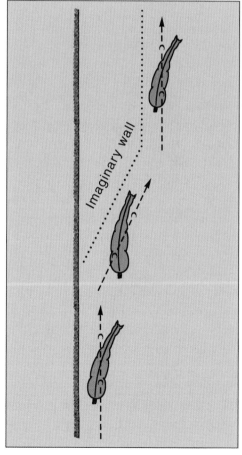

In this case, the angle of movement is about
40 degrees, which takes even the best dressage horse to his physical limits. A larger angle
such as K–P is no longer reasonable since
nature did not provide the horse with the
capacity to do the splits. Many a freestyle
rider should perhaps think about this.

The old common discussion of whether the
horse ought to move on three or four tracks
at half-pass, which angle of movement should
be obtained, if the forehand should lead or
not, and if the legs are crossing in the half-

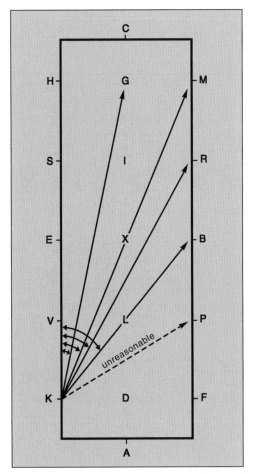

Fig. 70a: Half-pass possibilities with their directional points (G, M, R, B), angle of movement and line of movement.

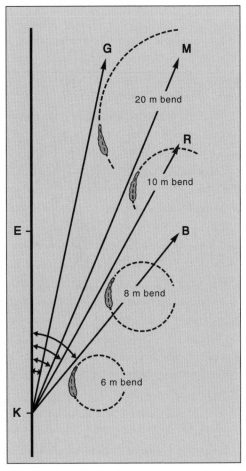

Fig. 70b: The angle of the line of movement produces the degree of difficulty of the half-pass. A bigger angle demands more lateral bend. Rhythm and Schwung must remain constant.

As long as this basic principle has been maintained by an evenness of lateral bending, the horse is moving correctly. The degree of difficulty of the half-pass depends exclusively, as previously mentioned, on the *angle of movement*: (Fig. 70a, b). If this angle is perhaps 30 degrees (K–R), the half-pass is of medium difficulty. If the angle is smaller (K–G or K–M) the movements are introductory exercises. If the angle is larger, approximately 40 degrees (K–B) it corresponds to the demands of the advanced levels where the utmost of bend is required (six-metre volte).

In the comparison of Figure 70a and Figure 71 it is evident that in the short arena (20 by 40 metres) the angles of movement are comparatively greater, thus the half-passes are more demanding than on a 20-by 60-metre arena. Just compare the angle of movement on the diagonal K–X–M.

The above cited two criteria are the most important factors of a half-pass. They answer the frequently asked questions:

Three or four tracks?

As long as the line of energy runs parallel to the line of movement, thus creating three tracks, the half-pass is most effective for thrust, *Schwung* and collection. However, above Third Level work (because of extreme lateral bend), the line of energy deviates more and more from being parallel to the line of movement. Thus the legs begin to cross over on four tracks. If however, the horse is moving on four tracks because of a lack of bend (the haunches fall out or lead), the purpose of the exercise is annulled.

What angle of the horse towards the line of movement?

The angle is a result if the basic principles of the half-pass (see above) are in place.

Should the legs cross or not?

"Crossing" can be an optical illusion. Whether the horse is crossing or not can be judged only from the end of the line of movement. But no judge sits there! The judge at C will always see a crossing, whether the horse is moving on three tracks (line of energy) or on four. Moving on four tracks the legs necessarily cross, which is correct as long as this occurs because of increased lateral bend and the two basic principles of the half pass are granted. Concluding, three points ought to be stressed once more. Firstly, lateral

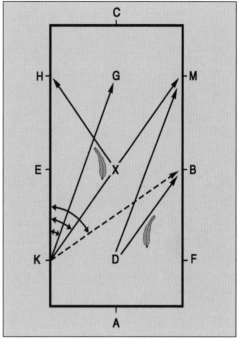

Fig. 71: Arena 20 x 40m
In comparison to the 20 x 60m arena, the angle of the movement is bigger, making the half-pass more difficult. For example: Line of movement K–M in an arena of 20 x 60 is of medium difficulty.
Line of movement K–M in 20 x 40 however is difficult
Line of movement K–B in 20 x 40 is unreasonable.

movements have no end in themselves. They are only means to a goal. Secondly, lateral movements should not only improve the quality of the basic gaits but the entire appearance of the horse should gain in beauty and radiance. If this does not occur the work has been faulty. Thirdly, lateral movements are most meaningful for developing Schwung and collection if the line of energy is assured. However, with all good intentions, we should not forget that the horse was designed to go forwards and lateral movements should only be a smaller part of our dressage work.

THE FLYING CHANGE OF LEAD

"In riding one never stops learning."

After successful basic training according to the Training Tree our young prospect should be ready for the flying lead change, that is the *flying* one, not some change of lead that untrained horses do when losing balance. This kind of lead change we observe quite often when observing hunters and jumpers in the show ring. Those horses at canter mostly change direction in two phases. At first with the front legs and later with the hind legs. This should not be criticized as a fault as long as the horse doesn´t stay in the disunited canter for more than two to three strides. But this is not a flying change! In a dressage test such a "change" scores less than satisfactory. Trainers who start the work on the flying change by using a cavalletti or ground pole at the end of a diagonal virtually *teach* the horse to change the wrong way. This kind of "late behind" change will be the reason later on for extreme problems with the correct flying change. Teaching the horse something new is a challenge anyway, so why not start things right? It is easier to plant something that is right in the horses brain than to take out something that is wrong.

In the correct lead change the horse cha-nges in *one phase* – in the phase of suspension.

This phase follows immediately after the inside front foot (Fig. 72a–d) has left the ground. For the left lead canter, that would be the left front. The longer the time of suspension, the rounder the canter and the better (and more meaningful) the change. The horse consequently changes airborne all four legs from the left lead to the right lead canter so the new outside (left) hind foot can take the weight and start the new right lead canter stride.

That sounds complicated – but it is not! Just make sure the canter is correct. The elements of the Training Tree must be confirmed and the strides should be round and lively. This is the only way your horse would be able to change on almost invisible aids.

But how to get to the flying change?

There are certainly horses that are born to be dancers. These horses, straight and balanced by nature, are rare. They submit to a sensitive rider right away without any problem. Not infrequently, such horses are sold for big money. Unfortunately, we do

Fig. 72 a) Left canter
Three legs on the ground. The outer (right) hind leaves the ground to go into the diagonal two legged support.

Fig. 72 b) *The canter ends with a single leg support on left fore. Rider changes aids.*

Fig. 72 c): *Horse in "moment of suspension" changes on all four legs.*

Fig. 72d): *Right canter lands on new outside (left) hind and goes on to three leg support.*

not tend tosee them later on among the top horses in dressage competitions. In most cases, because people took advantage of their talent, they became victims of their kind personalities and their willingness to please.

Our interest however, is focused on the normal riding horse that has finished its basic training and is on the way to Third Level.

Let us take another look at the Training Tree:

The well-known rule, "The fruit falls in your lap as soon as it is ripe", is specially meaningful for the flying change. Once the ten elements have been established properly and the horse already knows a bit about two-track work, for the experienced rider the flying change should not be a problem.

Whenever the horse does not respond or is resisting, it's because the horse is not ready for the change. In most of the cases there are deficits in the elements of basic training. For example, If there is not enough *Schwung* (Element 9), we must improve this. However we know from the Training Tree that *Schwung* depends on *Durchlässigkeit* (Element 8) and this cannot work without the horse being in Balance (Element 7). So in order to improve *Schwung* (Element 9), we need to work seriously on re-establishing and confirming all the previous elements.

Any attempt to demand the flying change without a solid basic foundation confuses or even frightens the horse and demonstrates poor horsemanship. It has nothing in common with the art of riding.

That is why only an experienced rider with an impeccable seat and a feel for the perfect timing should introduce the flying change to a young horse. An experienced rider knows when the horse is physically and mentally ready for it. Remaining on Second Level work for too long a time might establish the counter canter in a way that the flying change may become a problem.

A rider who is not familiar with the flying change should not try to teach this. He or she should rather develop the feel for the correct change on a well-trained schoolmaster. This corresponds to the well-proven principle that young horses learn from old rider´s and young riders learn from old horses.

Now, what aid do we apply for the flying change?

Once the horse is prepared as described before, an indication of a half-halt followed by a slight shifting of the riders position for the new lead should be enough to create the change.

In fact, the aid is the same as the one we are used to when asking for the canter from the walk or the trot: Half-halt, positioning seat and legs for the canter depart (inside seat bone light pressure downwards-forwards, inside leg asking at the girth, outside leg controlling one hand behind the girth, horse's head positioned to the inside, inside rein easing).

Since the old stride ends when the inside front takes the weight (Fig. 72b) the rider alters his legposition in this very moment to indicate the following lead change. This way the horse gets ready for the flying change. As soon as the inside front is about to leave the ground for the phase of suspension, the rider shifts his weight for the new lead and the horse will change (Fig. 72c). This may seem like a lot of theory, but knowing helps understanding and understanding helps developing the feel.

The *simple* change is the best exercise for preparing the flying change. The simple change is a transition from canter *through walk* to canter. The horse at the canter is straightened in the rails and sufficiently engaged from behind, which enables him to pick up a relaxed walk right away. After two to three clear steps he should strike off for the canter in the new lead.

The value of the movement lies in its correct execution. No trot step is allowed! The rider needs to concentrate on straightness, balance and timing. Simple changes carelessly executed are counterproductive rather than helpful for preparing the flying change.

Following the principle of making new things easy and understandable for the horse, we ride several simple changes exactly at the same point as where we later on want to ask for the flying change. This point as well as the direction of the track we are following is important for a successful first attempt. There are quite a few possibilities:

From the true canter:
- On a short or long diagonal, when arriving at the wall
- Figure eights on 20-metre circles, when changing direction
- Serpentines, when crossing centrerline
  Half-volte out of the corner, when arriving at the wall
  Half-volte into the corner, on the straight line before turning

From the counter canter:
- At the end of a shallow loop, before arriving at the wall
- At A, C, B, E or another letter (checkpoint) at the long side
- On the 20-metre circle, at one of the checkpoints

From the half-pass:
- There are many possibilities. However notice that the horse must take one stride straightforward before changing to the new lead.
  Rhythm! Impulsion! and counting on the third right beat:... right and right and right and *straight* and left and left and left . . .
  The straightened horse is able to change lead without effort.

OTHER CADMOS
BOOKS

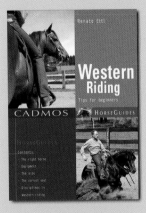

Renate Ettl
Western Riding

A perfect guide for beginners and those who wish to change to western riding.

**Paperback, 32 colour pages
ISBN 3-86127-933-9**

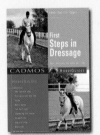

Anne-Katrin Hagen
First Steps in Dressage

The author describes lessons in serpentines, half-halt, basic paces with lengthening and leg-yielding.

**Paperback, 32 colour pages
ISBN 3-86127-932-0**

Anke Rüsbüldt
Vaccination and Worming of Horses

The author explains in detail why, how often and against what you should vaccinate and worm.

**Paperback, 32 colour pages
ISBN 3-86127-931-2**

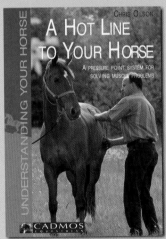

Chris Olson
A Hot Line to Your Horse

A Hot Line to Your Horse sets out an effective, easily comprehensible method which you can quickly master and use to enhance your horse's well-being and willingness to perform.

**Paperback, 80 colour pages
ISBN 3-86127-901-0**

For further information: Cadmos/The Editmaster Company
28 Langham Place Northampton NN2 6AA
Tel. 01604 715915 Fax: 06104 791209